Becoming a Better Writer

Using The Simple 6™

Prompts and Activities
Grades 3 - 6

By Kay Davidson

Pieces of Learning

CLC0409
ISBN 978-931334-98-3
© 2007 Pieces of Learning
www.piecesoflearning.com

Table of Contents

Chapter 1

What is The Simple 6™?

A Review of the Components

The Simple 6™: A Writing Rubric for Kids

Implementing the Simple 6™ Writing Program

Nine Week Review

Tips for Success

Chapter 1: The Simple 6™ A Writing Rubric for Kids

What is The Simple 6™?

Based on the academic standards and standardized writing assessments from across the country, The Simple 6™ is a student-friendly, simple analytic rubric. Originating in Indiana, The Simple 6™ evolved from frustration. While my elementary students were writing regularly and making continuous progress, they were not passing the standardized writing assessment that was given each year.

Across the United States, there is no single standard for exemplary writing. Every state is different, although most states offer a complex holistic rubric as their assessment tool. Each segment of the rubric has a phrase, a question, or a narrative that defines the point value. Assessment rubrics usually range from four to six points, including conventions or not. Some states add the points from two individual scorers or place the point value into a mathematical equation that will eventually become a total language arts score.

Scoring student writing with a complex holistic rubric is difficult. Why? Teachers give these reasons: *The language is too ambiguous. It is too difficult to understand exactly how to move from one level to the next. Scoring takes too much time. Choosing the line in the rubric that "best fits" doesn't always give a true assessment. I don't get it, so I just guess at the score, hoping to get close.* So what is accomplished by asking teachers to use complex holistic rubrics with which they do not feel comfortable?

Rubrics are designed for two purposes: to assess and/or to articulate expectations. However, the term rubric is so often tied to assessment that teachers often forget to use a rubric to guide expectations. Asking myself the question, *"What components of exemplary writing are seen in student writing samples that pass standardized assessments?"* was really the key to developing The Simple 6™. My main focus, however, was never to just "beat the test." Knowing and learning to focus on the components of exemplary writing made my students outstanding writers.

Why does it work?

The Simple 6™ works because students and teachers understand it. The language is clear, the order is developmentally progressive, and the scoring is relatively uncomplicated. Each component builds on the next, allowing students to master skills as they cumulatively review and work together to take control of their writing. Wherever you live, will find these elements of exemplary writing in your state scoring rubric.

Stick to the topic.	**Write descriptive sentences.**
Check for logical order.	**Use different sentence patterns.**
Include interesting words.	**Write for an audience.**

Just Simple 6™ It!

Stick to the Topic

Did I stick to the topic and not run away with other ideas?

Did I answer or address all the questions in the prompt?

If there were no questions, did I design my own questions?

Logical Order

Is there an introduction, or did I just dive right in?

Did I use a lead or hook to get my readers interested?

Is my conclusion strong? Is it more than one sentence?

Is the body organized, probably by the questions in the prompt?

Did each paragraph address a new question?

Interesting Words/Challenging Vocabulary

Did I eliminate overused words such as went, said, big, little, and good?

Did I go back and look for three more opportunities to use challenging vocabulary?

Are my new words used correctly?

Varied Sentence Patterns

Does my essay or story sound like a list?

Did I vary my sentence patterns, using questions, exclamations, and items in a series?

Did I write compound and/or complex sentences?

How many sentences start with prepositional, adverbial, or participial phrases?

Do my sentences have smooth transitions?

Descriptive Sentences

Did I create a vision for the reader that matches what I see in my head?

Did I use precise verbs?

Did I name people, places, and things with proper nouns?

Did I include adjectives – but not too many?

Did I appeal to the reader's senses?

Did I give several detailed examples?

Audience

Did I write for a specific audience?

Does my personality shine through my writing?

Does my tone match the prompt?

Name _____   Date _____

Title _____

The  Simple 6 ™ *A Writing Rubric for Kids*

Stick to the topic.
Check for logical order.
Include interesting words.
Use different sentence patterns.
Create descriptive sentences.
Write for an audience.

Ask these questions:
yes/no

_____   Did you **stick to the topic**, or did you run away with some other idea?

_____   Have you presented your thoughts in a **logical order** that included an inviting beginning and a strong conclusion?

_____   Have you gone back to look for opportunities to use **interesting words?**

_____   Did you use **different sentence patterns**, or does your story sound like a list?

_____   Does each paragraph have a topic sentence and supporting **detail sentences that are descriptive?**

_____   Did you write for an **audience?**
(original, lively, or another unique perspective appropriate for the prompt)

_____   TOTAL POINTS (How many did you answer yes?)

© Kay Davidson, 1998

Implementing The Simple 6™ Writing Program

Step 1. Collect baseline data before you begin.

What writing skills do your students currently have? Make copies of the writing samples and put them in a separate folder that you may refer to throughout the year. At the end of the year, return these copies with the final writing sample. This is the easiest and truest documentation of growth.

Step 2. Make student folders.

Make a folder for each student. All the Thursday/Friday prompt writing will be kept in this folder. Use a sheet on the front to track writing topics and their dates. (If students are truly writing about what you're doing in class, you should be able to see the highlights of your curriculum by reviewing writing topics.)

The nine week Simple 6™ plan consists of introducing or reviewing basic skills on Wednesday. On Thursday/Friday the teaching format is 60 minutes a day. Each 60-minute block is designed to include a lesson or motivation of some type, student interaction, and writing. (Detailed descriptions for the actual teaching of the nine week Implementation of The Simple 6™ can be found in Chapter 3 of Writing: The Simple 6™. This chapter includes a Thursday/Friday narrative, four follow-up activities, and standardized lesson plans for the narratives.)

Step 3. Use the "paper strategy" to organize writing time.

Students typically have a difficult time writing for 40 minutes or more. By helping them to manage each stage of writing, they use the time more wisely. In doing so, they write more thoroughly.

PLAN A	
Brainstorming	7 minutes
Organizing Ideas	8 minutes
Rough Draft	15 minutes
REST OVER NIGHT	
Revising/Editing	10 minutes
Final Draft	20 minutes

PLAN B	
Prompt Attack	15 minutes
Rough Draft	15 minutes
REST OVER NIGHT	
Revising/Editing	10 minutes
Final Draft	20 minutes

Nine Week Overview

Week 1:   Stick to the Topic
Instructional Focus:

> Write about the assigned topic only.
> Eliminate sentences that don't belong.
> Use the prompt questions to guide the body.

Week 2:   Logical Order
Instructional Focus:

> Retell well-known or familiar stories.
> Create "human sentences."
> Discuss transitional words and prepositional phrases.
> Define expectations for an inviting introduction and a
>   strong conclusion.

Week 3:   Interesting Words
Instructional Focus:

> Replace generic vocabulary with at least three
>   challenging words.
> Eliminate *went* and *said*.

Week 4:   Review, Share, and Revise
Instructional Focus:

> Review the elements of . . .
>   sticking to the topic
>   logical order
>   interesting words
> Think aloud as you model the writing process.
> Vary instructional strategies.
> Let students write in small groups.
> Get all students to a Score 3.

Week 5: **Different Sentence Patterns**
Instructional Focus:

List several sentences about the same topic.
Show variety by . . .
  changing word order
  including questions
  adding dialogue
  inserting exclamations
  adding prepositional phrases

Week 6: **Descriptive Sentences**
Instructional Focus:

Introduce strategies, such as inserting
  precise verbs
  proper nouns
  adjectives
  imagery
  literary devices

Week 7: **Audience**
Instructional Focus:

Analyze commercials to get students thinking
  about how to communicate with an audience.
Write advice column responses.
Talk about how adjusting tone helps to connect
  with an audience.

Week 8: **Peer Editing and Scoring**
Instructional Focus:

Show the entire Simple 6™ rubric   *or*
  each part of the process done well, one point will
  be given.
Practice scoring.

Week 9: **Creating a Score 6**
Instructional Focus:

Share samples of Score 6 exemplary writing.
Review the steps for revision.
Give students an opportunity to work together or
  alone to create a passing paper.
Use several formats for revision.

Detailed lesson plans for the implementation of The Simple 6™ writing program are found in Writing: The Simple ™6. Chapter 3, p. 38.

Tips for Success: Stay FOCUSED!! Use the DATA!!

1. Stay on a Thursday/Friday schedule. Keep the same time each day.

2. Establish a place for the writing folders.

3. Make sure students document writing tasks each week and keep samples in their folders.

4. Pay particular attention during informal observation. Is everyone participating?

5. Analyze the data each week.

6. Identify weaknesses by rubric component or individual student.

7. Conference with flexible skill groups and/or individuals weekly.

8. Praise students for their progress every step of the way.

9. Approach each lesson with enthusiasm and encouragement.

10. Step aside and let students take charge of the reviews and discussions.

11. Post a *Simple 6™* chart in your classroom, and refer to it every time students write.

12. Display writing samples and encourage students to share ideas with one another.

13. Celebrate your success.

From Writing: The Simple 6™ © Pieces of Learning

Chapter 2 After the First Nine Weeks:
Writing Across the Curriculum

Motivating Kids to Write

"Borrowing Time" in Other Subject Areas

The Picture Book Connection
Recommended Read Alouds for:
>   Stick to the Topic
>   Logical Order
>   Interesting Words
>   Different Sentence Patterns
>   Descriptive Sentences
>   Audience

The Writers' Workshop

How Do Prompts Fit into Today's Writing Curriculum?

Chapter 2   After the First Nine Weeks: Writing Across the Curriculum

What do I do after the nine weeks?

Once you've followed the nine-week implementation plan, get back to your "regular schedule" and just give students opportunities to write. They now have the skills to develop exemplary pieces of writing, and they need to practice using them – in all types of writing situations. Just as students should read every day, so should they write – and filling out a worksheet or completing a workbook page doesn't count as writing. It's easy now. They have the skills to get started. All you have to do is motivate them!

Motivating Kids to Write

What will we write about?
Topics that are:

- knowledge based
- imaginative
- imaginative
- appropriate for the age
- reflective, personal
- cross-curricular
- chosen by teachers (literature, content, pictures, events, people)

- fun
- imaginative
- authentic
- chosen by students   (interest)
- of various genre

How will we do it?

We will work:

- alone
- in small groups, in teams, or with partners
- together--jigsawing ideas or contributing chapters
- in class, during Writers' Workshop
- with colored pencils, pens, markers, and the computer
- with graphic organizers and story maps
- on research to get more information
- on various types of poetry as well as prose
- on writing in other subjects

What will the product look like when it's finished?

The piece might:
- be written or printed on unusual paper
- be illustrated
- turn into a play
- become a bound book
- be sent in for publication
- be given as an oral presentation
- be displayed for others to read
- become a poster or a shape book
- be contributed to the class or school newspaper
- be saved in a journal

How do I schedule this into my day?

The Thursday/Friday plan for one hour of writing a day is already in place. After the first nine weeks students have the skills, so analysis of their writing will now determine the skills that need to be reinforced. In a nine-week grading period, use the Thursday/Friday format every other week (for instance weeks 2, 4, 6, and 8). On those specific weeks possibly present a traditional lesson based on weaknesses from the Student and Class Analysis Chart (pages 155 -156) and take writing up to the rough draft, review a revision strategy the next day as the lesson, let students work together in small groups, and revise, edit, and complete rough drafts. This is the same format used during implementation.

On one of those four weeks, you might put students in a standardized assessment simulation. They would come into class on Thursday, see the prompt for the first time, and write for 55 minutes. Score all papers after school, (It takes about an hour for a class of about 25 students) and put the mini rubric face down in the bottom of the writing folder. The next day have another student score the paper, using the mini rubric. They would also place it face down on the bottom of the writing folder. Thirdly, the student would score his own paper with the mini rubric. Then she would take out the other two from her folder. Lining them up, the student gets immediate feedback from three sources.

What about the other weeks? Just write! Give students time to write about individual topics or interests in a Writers' Workshop format, or help students write across the curriculum. The most important thing to remember is that students should write for different purposes, write in all subject areas, and write all throughout the day! Borrow writing time from other subjects, and remember to bring writing to your lessons!

"Borrowing Time" in Other Subject Areas
How can I "bring writing" to the other subjects I teach?

Social Studies

Writing about math gives students opportunities to explain how they think. They struggle with this! While most teachers think that there isn't enough time in the day for students to write during math, there are several ways to "quick-write" that are effective.

- Prove that 2 + 2 = 4
- Show me why $\frac{1}{2}$ of 6 is 3
- Tell me what addition (or subtraction, or multiplication, or division) means. Give an example.
- Solve this word problem. Explain how you got your answer.
- Solve this two-step problem. Explain which strategies you used and tell why.
- Write a paragraph summarizing what you learned by reading this graph.
- Explain how you got your answer to the first homework problem.
- Write a paragraph explaining the concept we learned today.

Science

Writing during a science lab is what scientists do! Of course, you have to be willing to let students engage in science labs before you can get them to write about them. It's another one of those activities that should definitely be included in your weekly schedule – same time, same day, every week.

- Explain how frogs are different from toads.
- Answer this essay question thoroughly in a well-developed paragraph.
- Make predictions based on this research.
- Generalize your findings after doing today's experiment.
- Design a plan for gathering data. Explain it in detail.
- Explain the process of photosynthesis (or another scientific process).
- Explain why there are earthquakes.
- Develop a hypothesis prior to doing the experiment today.
- After the experiment, write about whether your hypothesis was correct or incorrect.
- Draw a diagram, and explain how this invention works.
- Write a paragraph that restates the scientific facts you learned.

Social Studies

Social studies is an obvious place to write. These writings will enhance the knowledge base you are building in geography, history, and current events.

- ➤ Recap this historical event in a short essay.
- ➤ Create a brochure that entices me to come to this geographic location.
- ➤ Write a journal entry about this famous event.
- ➤ Summarize the main points in this speech.
- ➤ Write a news article about a major event that happened in the world this week.
- ➤ Create a time line that depicts the events during this era. Add a short narration.
- ➤ Write a concise paragraph about the contributions this person made.
- ➤ Predict what the world would be like if this discovery had not been made.
- ➤ Use the information you learned about this famous person, and write a biographical fiction piece about him.
- ➤ Write a paragraph about what you learned today.
- ➤ Write a note to me telling me what you still don't understand.

Fine Arts

When students go to music and art classes with "specialists" for a limited amount of time, it's not always practical to expect these teachers to include writing in their already over-loaded schedule. There are many things you can do in the classroom, however, to rein-force the importance of writing in the fine arts areas.

- ➤ Write a paragraph that reflects the mood of this piece of music.
- ➤ Using metaphor, compare yourself to a musical instrument.
- ➤ Compare the styles of two musical groups.
- ➤ Summarize the story in this musical.
- ➤ Write a paragraph about this musician.
- ➤ Write about what might have inspired the artist to paint this picture.
- ➤ Tell why you think these illustrations are effective in this picture book.
- ➤ Write a descriptive paragraph based on this picture.
- ➤ Critique this piece of artwork.
- ➤ Explain the art medium that you enjoy most.
- ➤ Write a persuasive letter to me convincing me that we should paint in class more often.
- ➤ Write an imaginary story from this famous piece of art.

Computer Lab

Technology is here! If you're still avoiding the inevitable, it's time to get on board. Whether you feel confident in teaching students to become more technologically advanced or not, it's your responsibility to make sure that students have as much experience with computers and technological enhancements as possible. The means in which we communicate with one another has changed drastically in the past 10 years. Have you changed with the times?

- Type your spelling words in two columns.
- Type your vocabulary words. Use your computer to find the definitions.
- Type your spelling sentences. (Don't forget to include this week's grammar requirement.)
- Type your paragraph. Use the tab key to indent. Center the title.
- Use your computer to find synonyms for these words.
- Have young students read their stories to you. Type them in 24-26 points, let them choose their font, and add their names as the authors.
- Create short, imaginative stories on the computer. Add clip art.
- Write a news article using a publishing program.
- Type in various sizes, fonts, and colors.
- Write an email.
- Use a search engine to find information for your writing.

Physical Education

If I had to choose one subject where students would not write, it would be physical education. I would carry my physical education issues and ideas into health, because I feel that most students lack enough physical activity to keep them healthy and active. Too many are overweight, don't exercise, can't take turns, won't follow game rules, and have poor sportsmanship. Given the choice, my students will participate in physical activity and write in the other subject areas. Here are a few ideas to carry over into health or into the classroom.

- Write about the rules of this game.
- Tell why being a good sport is a positive character trait.
- Explain how to play the game you learned today.
- Write a paragraph telling how today's argument could have been avoided.
- Write a plan for a healthy diet.
- Write a paragraph about dinnertime at your house.

Language Arts

The language arts block is the most obvious place for teachers to plan writing activities, but it shouldn't be all-inclusive. As students read and work with words, it is natural for them to want to write. Eliminate worksheets!

- Write your spelling words in alphabetical order in your best cursive handwriting.
- Write spelling sentences for the 5 toughest words. (include specific grammar focus)
- Review grammatical chunks such as prepositional phrases. Improve simple sentences by adding them effectively.
- Review literary devices such as alliteration, onomatopoeia, simile, metaphor, and imagery.
- Create lists of things you are interested in writing about.
- Get ideas for writing from picture books.
- Reflect on literature.
- Practice asking and writing high-level questions.
- Make a list of things you wonder about. Then write about them.
- Make a list of things you already know about. Then write about them.
- Make a list of things you are interested in learning more about. Then find out more about them.
- Write about characters with whom you feel a connection.
- Write about dreams you have.
- Make a list of words you like the sound of.
- Reflect on your connections with stories or characters.
- Write about past life experiences.
- Write poetry.
- Create imaginary characters or events.
- Learn to be analytical as well as creative.
- Write simple definitions so you can learn to be specific in your thinking.
- Collect words in Word Banks.
- Make notes to yourself about grammar questions you want to ask your teacher.
- Write a novel, one chapter at a time.
- Read the introduction from two books. Explain why one is better than the other.
- After reading, write about the strategy the author used to end the story.
- Write a new ending to a story.
- Write about how a story might have ended differently if the characters had interacted with one another in a different way.
- Write about the character that you respect most in the story.
- Give your opinion about this book.

The Picture Book Connection:
Text to Self . . . Text to Text . . .
Text to World

Making connections to events in life is how writers get ideas. There are many ways to build this knowledge and experience base, even with young writers. What better way to connect than through your reading?

Text to Self: As students read, they make connections to real life experiences. An illustration, a story idea or theme, a sentence, or even a word can bring memories to the surface that will motivate students to write something they know about and care about. Have I had any of the experiences that are happening in this book? Am I like any of these characters? Does this book remind me of anything that has happened in my own life? Do I have opinions about this book based on what I already know?

Text to Text: As students read more, they broaden their experience and knowledge base. They "know" characters, authors, and their styles. They begin to develop preferences for specific types of literature or read all the books by a certain author. It is with this emersion in literature that students begin to make connections to other texts as they read. How is this book like the last book I read by this author? The theme of this book is the same as two others I have read, yet they are very different from one another. How?

Text to World: Students start at a very young age in their "me" world. As they grow and mature, they expand their experiences and focus from me – to family – to school and neighborhood – to friends – to community – to region – to world. They begin to make connections with day-to-day experiences, current events, and nonfiction reading . . . *What's happening in my world today? How will it affect me? Do I care about it? Can I change it?*

Current trends in literacy instruction focus more on preparing students to read than ever before. Discussing what the story might be about, making predictions, taking a picture walk-through, and sharing connections to real life experiences are a major part of reading instruction – not just the short introduction before reading a story. Where literal comprehension questions were historically used to determine whether a student could actually read and understand the text, they are now more a part of the preparation for reading the story – allowing students to focus more on higher levels of thinking, such as reflection and analysis, during and after reading.

Taking it a step further, students are encouraged to journal as they read. These journals are not just ideas or notes to remind us of facts that will be needed to retell the story later (or write a book report). Because students are so familiar with the lower level "facts" of the story, they are now free to reflect, connect, wonder about, and imagine – and they do this in special journals that are designated for this type of writing.

Here are ideas to spark reflection and response rather than literal summarization. You may want to duplicate this, have students cut it out, and glue it to the inside of their reading response journal to remind of them of different ways they might consider responding to literature.

Write a personal reaction to the story. Make a connection with one of the characters. Comment on how a character changed. Before you finish make predictions about the story. Write a descriptive sentence from the book and tell about it. Relate this story to your own life. In a picture book, comment on the pictures only. Compare two books by the same author. Make a list of questions you wonder about as you read. Give your personal reactions to certain parts of the story. Refer to a specific entry as a major event in the story. Comment on the author's style. Give reasons for not finishing a particular book.

Learning the Craft

Applying what is already known is just one of the connections students make as they read. Students should now, with your help, start recognizing how memorable stories come together. What does exemplary writing look like? What do I like about this author's style that reminds me of myself? What do I admire about this author's style that I might want to learn more about? Does this story have a great beginning? How does the story end? What is the overall structure that makes the events easy to remember? What strategies are used by this author to make me get a clear picture of what the characters are doing and feeling? What literary devices (such as simile, metaphor, humor, repetition, onomatopoeia, and imagery) are used by this author to make the story entertaining? Are there any new words in this story that I need to make note of?

Reading picture books to students is a great motivator and instructional tool for writers of all ages – not just primary students. As we model lessons and instructional strategies as we teach skills, so should we point out those model lessons and examples that have been provided to us by the authors of children's picture books.

The Simple 6™ takes all the components of exemplary writing and provides a framework for students to examine closely the author's tone and style. As they become more proficient in analyzing the writing of others, these skills naturally carry over into their own writing and revision. Consider this short list of strategies for bringing The Simple 6™ to a read-aloud discussion.

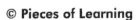

As you read aloud to your class. . .
Integrate . . . focus . . . discuss . . . make connections

Stick to the Topic
1. Summarize the story.
2. Discuss main idea / details.

Logical Order
1. Choose 5 students to retell the story. BMMME
2. Walk through the pictures *after* reading.
3. Draw comic strips of the story.
4. Identify the strategy for the conclusion.

Interesting Words
1. Collect the three best words from a book.
2. Listen for precise *verbs*.

Varied Sentence Patterns
1. Practice question – answer.
2. Listen for exclamations.
3. Identify repetitive patterns.

Descriptive Sentences
1. Point out and discuss descriptive language.
2. Help students make connections to real life.
3. Ask students to illustrate a part of the story, but you really MUST teach the drawing skills.
4. Focus on particular characteristics of characters, especially animals.

Audience
1. Point out books written in first person.
2. Read with expression and enthusiasm.

Don't overdo it. Choose your focus before you read.

The following lists are books that you might consider using as you teach and review and model each of the 6 components in The Simple 6™. There are an infinite number of possible choices, but these suggestions will at least get you started. They are divided into categories, but many of the books have more than one strength. There is also space to write in your own preferences. Any book you choose will fit into one or more categories of The Simple 6™.

STICK TO THE TOPIC

Books chosen for this Simple 6™ component have an easily identifiable theme or main idea. In addition, books in this category were not strong in just one of the other components.

APPRECIATION

The A+ Custodian, by Louise Borden (2004)
I like the language, I like the sentence patterns, I like the descriptions, but mostly I just like this story. It s the story of how the Early Birds made sure that their friend and custodian, Mr. Carillo, was noticed and appreciated by everyone.

CULTURAL DIFFERENCES

How My Parents Learned to Eat, by Ina Friedman (1984)
When parents are from two cultures, it's not unusual to combine traditions. In this case, it's whether to eat with chopsticks or with a knife and fork!

DEDICATION / HARD WORK

The Royal Bee, by Frances and Ginger Park (2000)
A young Korean boy named Song-ho wins The Royal Bee, even though boys of his meager background are not ordinarily allowed to attend The Sodang School.

Riptide, by Frances Weller (1990)
Zachary's dog, Riptide, won't give up until he is accepted as the cape's 19th lifeguard. This true story also has an exceptional introduction for young writers.

FAMILY

The Babe and I, by David Adler (1999)
In the midst of the Great Depression in 1932, Babe Ruth's home runs help a boy sell papers so he can get his family through the hard times.

The Patchwork Quilt, by Valerie Flournoy (1985)
This heartwarming story tells how a family all pitches in to complete Grandma's masterpiece – the patchwork quilt made from pieces of fabric belonging to everyone in the family.

Leah's Pony, by Elizabeth Friedrich (1996)
A young girl sells her beloved horse so she can purchase her father's tractor, which is up for auction.

The Sunday Outing, by Gloria Pinkney (1994)
A young black girl named Ernestine longs to ride a train. When she is invited to visit the relatives in Robeson County, everyone in the family gives something up so she can get there on the train.

When Lightning Comes in a Jar, by Patricia Polacco (2002)
This is a great example of a personal narrative that calls back the memories of a family reunion and the night all the cousins caught lightning in a jar.

FRIENDSHIP / KINDNESS

Enemy Pie, by Derek Munson (2000)
This is a very creative story about how enemy pie can turn your worst enemy into your best friend. Told in first person.

Fishing Day, by Andrea Pinkney (2003)
Mama and Reenie spend every Saturday morning fishing. When a white boy and his father fish in the same spot, Reenie breaks the rules of the Jim Crow South and offers him kindness.

IMAGINATION

Just a Dream, by Chris Van Allsburg (1990)
Walter, who isn't very environmentally conscious, dreams about what the future will be like. When he returns to the present, he has learned to appreciate the environment as well as the peace and beauty in nature.

LONELINESS

The Old Woman Who Named Things, by Cynthia Rylant (1996)
An old woman who has outlived all her friends is reluctant to become attached to a stray dog. However, when he doesn't show up one day, she drives Betsy to the dog pound and brings Lucky home.

I Can Hear the Sun, by Patricia Polacco (1996)
Fondo lives in the settlement-house building, where they keep homeless and unwanted children. He befriends a blind goose and, in the end, flies away with the migrating geese so he won't be sent to a special school.

YOUR FAVORITES. . .

LOGICAL ORDER

Expository or narrative, these books have a definite sense of order. Which have the best introductions and/or conclusions?

Butterfly House, by Eve Bunting (1999)
This beautifully illustrated book tells the story of a young girl who, with the help of her grandfather, cares for a larva until it is time for it to turn into a butterfly. While I appreciate the vivid descriptions, I focused on logical order for the steps of metamorphosis. There is also a page at the end of the book that gives students the specific steps for raising a butterfly.

First Day Jitters, by Julie Danneberg (2000)
What a great surprise ending! The person with the jitters on the first day of school is not the child as we suspect throughout the story . . . it's the teacher!

Wilfrid Gordon McDonald Partridge, by Mem Fox (1985)
This book has many outstanding literary qualities, but I focused on logical order because of the repetitious nature of the introduction and conclusion. The sentence patterns also contribute to a story that is easy to read, but packed with meaning.

Ice Cream: The Full Scoop, by Gail Gibbons (2006)
This nonfiction book about the discovery and making of ice cream is loaded with facts and drawings that take you through the process. I particularly like this book because of the ease in which you can see the topic sentence and how it leads to the development of a paragraph.

The 5,000-Year-Old Puzzle, by Claudia Logan (2002)
Solve the mystery of ancient Egypt as you travel with Will Hunt and his family. This factual book, written in journal fashion, is informative as well as entertaining.

The Black Snowman, by Phil Mendez (1989)
The introduction takes the reader back in time to a lonely grass hut in western Africa, telling the tale of the magic kente. Present-day Jacob Miller learns to believe in himself and the greatness of his heritage when a magic black snowman helps him save his brother from a burning building. This is one of those stories that ends with the feeling that another story is forthcoming.

Dinosaur Dream, by Dennis Nolan (1990)
Wilbur takes a walk back through time, returning an Apatosaurus named Gideon to his family.

The Official m & m's History of Chocolate, by Red, Yellow, Green, and Blue (2001)
I like this book for logical order because so few entertaining books have timelines, but don't sell this one short! It's loaded with outstanding sentence patterns, and the m & m characters' comments make a direct connection to the audience.

Shrek, by William Steig (1990)
I always consider William Steig to be the guru of challenging vocabulary, but I chose this book for its illustrious introduction and the humorous conclusion. This is a tale of Shrek, who is searching for an ugly princess. When he sighs "apple strudel" and she coos "cocka-doodoodle", he knows she's the one! Various parts of this story are also spiced up with great verse!

The Journey, by Sara Stewart (2001)
A young Amish girl records her first visit to the city in her diary. The first person connection is outstanding as she vividly tells about her feelings and observations as she ventures from the Amish community for the first time. Organized by date, her narrative gives students an example of a unique way to structure a story.

The Sweetest Fig, by Chris Van Allsburg (1993)
This is the story of a greedy, fussy dentist. One day an old woman pays him with two magic figs instead of money. He is furious, but he soon learns that whatever he dreams will come true. Find out how this selfish man turns into a dog rather than becoming the richest man in the world. This author sets the stage well in the first paragraph and has a great surprise ending.

The Wretched Stone, by Chris Van Allsburg (1991)
The crew aboard the Rita Anne has turned into monkeys! Rich with descriptive language and challenging vocabulary, this imaginative tale is shared day by day through the Captain's journal.

YOUR FAVORITES . . .

INTERESTING WORDS
(Challenging Vocabulary)

These authors use vocabulary "outside the box" for a particular age level. While the words are known and meanings may be determined through context, there are great examples of challenging vocabulary throughout the text.

The Princess and the Pizza, by Mary Jane and Herm Auch (2002)
The fairy tale takes a twist when the king decides he wants to be a wood carver. That means his daughter is no longer a princess, which she begins to miss desperately. She enters a contest to marry Prince Drupert. Loaded with challenging vocabulary, descriptions, and voice, this hilarious book is very entertaining.

Between Earth and Sky, by Joseph Bruchac (1996)
This impressive book tells the legends of the Native American sacred places. Using descriptive language and challenging vocabulary, it also tells about the Seventh Direction, the one that helps people to live their lives in a good way.

Miss Alaineus, A Vocabulary Disaster, by Debra Frasier (2000)
The motivation for this book came from making mistakes, which is something we all do. When Sage misses school on Vocabulary Day, Starr gives her the list of vocabulary words over the phone. The last word on the list is miscellaneous, which Sage misinterprets as Miss Alaineus. This error makes for a unique story about a classroom that is entrenched in vocabulary development.

Will's Quill (or How a Goose Saved Shakespeare), by Don Freeman (1975)
This old-fashioned tale takes place in London town. A country goose is treated kindly by none other than William Shakespeare. He returns the favor, giving him a quill to complete the play, *A Mid Summer Night's Dream*. Interesting dialect and challenging vocabulary.

Looking Out for Sarah, by Glenna Lang (2001)
The author describes the responsibilities of a Seeing Eye dog. You'll find great use of vocabulary and descriptive sentences.

Emma and the Silk Train, by Julie Lawson (1998)
Exceptional vocabulary is used in this story about the speed of the silkers, the value of silk, and the day a silk banner saved Emma's life.

The Remarkable Farkle McBride, by John Lithgow (2000)
A young musical prodigy discovers that conducting music makes him happier than playing any of the numerous musical instruments he has played in the past. The use of onomatopoeia and verse make this an appealing story.

My Rows and Piles of Coins, by Tololwa Mollel (1999)
Saruni longs for a bicycle so he can help his mother carry the loads to the market. This book has outstanding vocabulary and particularly noticeable precise verbs. It's also a great story about helping others.

The Wump World, by Bill Peet (1970)
The Wumps lived very peacefully in their little world until they were invaded by Pollutions from millions of miles away. This highly descriptive book has great vocabulary choices.

The Amazing Bone, by William Steig (1976)
Pearl and her new friend (a small talking bone) outwit a band of robbers and use the bone's magic words to escape from a fox. He then becomes part of Pearl's family. As always, Steig uses exceptional vocabulary and outstanding descriptions.

Sylvester and the Magic Pebble, by William Steig (1969)
One of my all-time favorites, you can always count on William Steig to use outstanding vocabulary as he tells his tale. In this book, Sylvester finds a magic pebble and wishes for the wrong things.

Big Bad and a Little Bit Scary, by Wade Zahares (2001)
Challenging vocabulary and descriptive sentences spice up this book of poems about animals.

YOUR FAVORITES. . .

DIFFERENT SENTENCE PATTERNS

Books that have a question-answer format, short exclamatory sentences, use of transition words, or a repetitive (sometimes even rhyming) pattern help students to focus on the use of different sentence patterns to eliminate "list-like" writing.

Right Here on this Spot, by Sharon Hart Addy (1999)
This highly descriptive book uses short but powerful sentence patterns to take you on the path of the Paleo Indians.

The Wall, by Eve Bunting (1999)
A little boy and his father come to visit the Vietnam Veterans Memorial so the little boy can find his grandfather's name. I like this book because of the appropriateness of the sentence structure. It's just right for elementary students, even though the boy in the story is probably in first or second grade.

How does the Wind Walk? by Nancy White Carlstrom (1993)
This book is loaded with literary devices, but I particularly like it for emphasizing sentence patterns. Each section begins with a question and is followed by a descriptive answer. It is further enhanced by the repetitive nature of the text format.

Fiddlin' Sam, by Marianna Dengler (1999)
This is a heartwarming story about passing down the gift of music. A repetitive pattern and a story that flows makes this one you'll want to read more than once.

Louisa May and Mr. Thoreau's Flute, by Julie Dunlap (2002)
I just appreciate the way this story flows. It is the story of Louisa May Alcott and her fond memories of her teacher, Henry David Thoreau.

Hello, Harvest Moon, by Ralph Fletcher (2003)
Focusing on sentence patterns seems to diminish the overall quality of this book. Its rich descriptions and challenging vocabulary make it seem real, but its sentence patterns make it unique.

The Sunsets of Miss Olivia Wiggins, by Lester Laminack (1998)
Miss Olivia's daughter and grandson visit her in the nursing home. The vividly descriptive text follows a repetitive pattern as she recalls important events throughout her life.

Punctuation Takes a Vacation, by Robin Pulver (2003)
Even though the text of this book is written for younger children, the message for upper elementary students is clear. If we forget to use punctuation, nothing will make sense. It's a great story with a very clear-cut message. The last page in the book also has a simple list of the punctuation rules that will be a great review or addition to a writer's notebook.

Skippyjon Jones, by Judy Schachner (2003)
This book has examples of so many different kinds of sentence patterns. You'll find simple sentences, complex sentences, one-word exclamations, and examples of dialogue, song, and rhyme. Add to it a little Spanish flavor, and you've got yourself one entertaining book for kids of all ages.

Hooray for Diffendoofer Day! by Dr. Seuss (1998)
This last book by Dr. Seuss tells about a very unique school where teachers teach children, not standards. When a test unexpectedly comes along, these students get the highest scores around. Written in verse, filled with whimsical descriptions and challenging vocabulary, this is a grand finale for Dr. Seuss.

The World that We Want, by Kim Toft (2005)
This nonfiction book about the importance of taking care of our world has a repetitive, cumulative, "House that Jack Built" format. The message of preventing the destruction of wildlife habitats is shared through vividly descriptive sentences, colorful illustrations, and challenging vocabulary!

Our Old House, by Susan Vizurraga (1997)
In a style that resembles free verse, a young girl finds treasures in the old house into which she and her family have just moved. The house used to belong to someone named Ruth, and one day Ruth actually drops by. I liked the style of the words on the page as well as the repetitive nature of the story.

The Velveteen Rabbit, by Margery Williams (1958)
This classic tells of a boy who loved his stuffed rabbit. When he gets scarlet fever the rabbit must be thrown away, but it is saved by the nursery magic fairy and becomes real. Always a favorite.

YOUR FAVORITES. . .

DESCRIPTIVE SENTENCES

Look for the strategies for writing more descriptive sentences: precise verbs, proper nouns, adjectives, sensory description, imagery, and other literary devices to help you find other books that are exemplary examples of descriptive language. (Don't forget the importance of non-narrative books to model verbal communication using the same strategies!)

ZOOM, by Istvan Banyai (1995)
This unusual book starts with a close-up picture of a rooster's comb. As the "lens" moves back, the story includes more and more details. This unique non-narrative takes you from a close up of a rooster's comb to the depths of outer space.

Things that are MOST in the World, by Judi Barrett (2001)
This quick-read book of superlatives has outstanding comparisons and realistic pictures.

Togo, by Robert Blake (2002)
This gripping tale of courage tells the story of the 1925 serum run in Alaska, an event commemorated annually by the Iditarod Race. Its precise verbs and descriptive language fill the reader with vivid images of courage and strength.

The Sea Chest, by Toni Buzzeo (2002)
This is a tale of a ship lost at sea and a little baby girl sent to shore in a treasure chest. The descriptive language and the style used by the author are absolutely magnificent.

Basket Moon, by Barbara Cooney (1999)
There are many examples of sensory perception in this book about a basket maker and his family.

The Worry Stone, by Marianna Dengler (1996)
This book has a story within a story within a story! Amanda worries about a friendless boy as she reflects on her own childhood and her remembrances of her grandfather. As she recalls his telling of the legend of the Worry Stone, she knows how she will help the boy in the park. The descriptive sentences and vocabulary enrich the text. The watercolor illustrations are outstanding.

When the Whippoorwill Calls, by Candice Ransom (1995)
This vividly descriptive book tells the tale of a family forced from its home in the Blue Ridge Mountains when the land is dedicated for a National Park.

Time Flies, by Eric Rohmann (1994)
This non-narrative book encourages students to describe their own thoughts and visions as they critically examine each oil painting of prehistoric times.

Hello Ocean, by Pam Munoz Ryan (2001)
Wow! There are so many examples of descriptive language in this short book about a day at the beach. Onomatopoeia, personification, metaphor, and imagery emerge from these lines of verse.

Boy, Can He Dance, by Eileen Spinelli (1993)
Tony's father would like him to follow family tradition and become a chef. All Tony wants to do, though, is dance! Use of precise verbs, onomatopoeia, color, and word placement on the page make this a winner!

The Stranger, by Chris Van Allsburg (1986)
While this book is very descriptive and has impressive illustrations that move with the story, readers leave the story with more questions than answers. Imaginative and mysterious, this story will inspire students to think and wonder.

June 29, 1999, by David Wiesner (1992)
As part of a science research project, Holly launches vegetable seedlings into the ionosphere. After several weeks, they return to Earth in massive sizes, just as she expected. She can't figure out, though, why other types of vegetables are appearing in parts of the country that were not included in her experiment. The vocabulary is challenging, but I particularly like this book for its choice of precise verbs. To top it off, there's a surprise ending!

YOUR FAVORITES. . .

AUDIENCE / VOICE

Connecting with the audience has two parts: writing in a tone that is appropriate for the story, and bringing personality and insight to the text that really moves the reader.

The Pain and The Great One, by Judy Blume (1974)
Written as free verse, the two stories in this book express the frustrations a sister has over her younger brother and her older sister. Written in first person, there's no doubt about how the writer feels!

The Storm, by Marc Harshman (1995)
We get a real sense of how Jonathan feels about being confined to a wheelchair when he must cope with being alone during a tornado that cuts through the family farm. The text also has great examples of different sentence patterns, challenging words, and excellent descriptions.

Just Add One Chinese Sister, by Patricia McMahon (2005)
This well-written, moving story about a family that adopts a little girl from China includes a side journal written by her older brother. You'll probably need a tissue to get through this one!

The Rag Coat, by Lauren Mills (1991)
Minna wears a new coat to school that is made of clothing scraps from the Quilting Mothers. The other students make fun of her until she begins to tell the story behind each scrap. Told in first person, this is a moving story about sadness and friendship.

Cow, by Jules Older (1997)
This book is loaded, and I mean loaded, with examples of connecting with the audience! Older writes in a style that makes voice just pop out of the pages for students and teachers alike! If I had could choose only one author to model voice, this would unquestioningly be the one. Logical order is a strong second choice here!

Pig, by Jules Older (2004)
I LOVE this author's unique, entertaining style. If you're looking for examples of using voice to connect with the audience, read this comical, informative book about pigs. I dare you not to smile!

So You Want to Be President? by Judith St. George (2000)
This entertaining book gives kids lots of information about former presidents. An excellent example of compare and contrast, its friendly, conversational style appeals to upper elementary students. Regarding sentence patterns, I would ask students to identify pages that need to be improved because of list-like transitions.

It's Disgusting – and We Ate It! by James Solheim (1998)
Written especially for kids, this informative book compares and contrasts, questions and answers, and simply gives tons of information about the foods we eat. Written in a subtly humorous style, this author clearly shows how you can report information in an entertaining way.

Rumpelstiltskin's Daughter, by Diane Stanley (1997)
In this unusual twist on the traditional Rumpelstiltskin, the people of the kingdom get warm, gold clothing, the homeless get shelter, the moat comes down, the guards are fired, and Rumpelstiltskin's daughter becomes Prime Minister!

BOING! by Sean Taylor (2004)
This quick read has it all! It's loaded with voice, has outstanding descriptions, and is spiced up with just the right amount of challenging vocabulary! Students will particularly like this one as a source because of its brevity.

Alexander, Who Used to Be Rich Last Sunday, by Judith Viorst (1978)
With combinations of short and long sentences, Alexander has a knack for connecting with the reader. This story leaves no doubt in your mind about how Alexander is feeling at any given moment!

Earrings, by Judith Viorst (1990)
This is a hilarious story about a girl who is trying to convince her parents to let her get her ears pierced. Spiced with short repetitions and more complex persuasions, we feel the wheels turning in this girl's head. She won't stop until she gets what she wants!

YOUR FAVORITES. . .

The Writers' Workshop
Writing for the Sake of Writing

It is said that if you can't give a Writers' Workshop an hour every day, don't bother. Forcing teachers to make that kind of commitment on a daily basis is why some teachers just don't do it at all. Consistency, not time allotment, is the key. Doing anything regularly in small amounts is better than having to commit to huge amounts of time that you know just don't exist every day. In addition, participating in many different kinds of writing every day is important, because all students don't learn the same way, think the same way, or enjoy doing the same types of things. Whenever teachers get tunnel vision in a single theory or program, they limit their students' opportunities to find their individual strengths.

It takes an outstanding teacher to oversee effectively a Writers' Workshop every day. This teacher knows each student's strengths, weaknesses, and interests.

- She knows at what stage of the writing process the student is working, how long he has been there, and if it's time to encourage him to move on to something else.
- She knows which books might spur this student's interests and which authors model techniques he would be interested in trying.
- She knows each student's style and could probably identify a piece of writing without a name on it.
- She manages time, space, books, skills, topics, levels of efficiency, interests, writing samples, and assessment.
- She asks rather than tells.
- She motivates rather than threatens.
- She assists rather than does.
- She conferences rather than writes in red.
- She praises and builds confidence rather than criticizes.
- On any given day, if asked, she can tell you what each student is working on and what her focus is for assistance and guidance.

How many teachers do you know who can honestly do this effectively? Not many – and that's why it's so important to make time for many types of writing in the classroom.

Teachers who encourage students to be life-long writers provide students with. . .

Places to Write that are sometimes away from their desks

Things to Write With or Supplies other than pencils

Surfaces to Write On that sometimes differ from notebook paper

Ideas to Write About that shouldn't always come from the teacher

Peers to Critique and Offer Suggestions about their Writing and that means allowing students to talk to one another

Fewer Worksheets
(In fact, a great goal for you to have is to be the teacher in your building who runs the fewest copies. Setting a goal of one worksheet per day is not unrealistic. With 25 students, that's still 125 copies a week or 4750 copies per school year. That still comes out to 10 reams of paper per year per teacher.)

IDEAS + OPPORTUNITIES + SUPPLIES = GREAT STORIES!

How Do Prompts Fit into Today's Writing Curriculum?

For many educators, they don't. The focus on writing in today's literacy models is to let students do their own thing, writing about personal topics of interest – in their own way and in their own time. Certainly, prompt writing appears to be everything that writing in a Writers 'Workshop environment is not. However, while many individuals don't believe that prompt writing is "authentic writing," there are some valid reasons for teaching students how to write to specific prompts. These are emphasizing structure, using imagination, simulating standardized testing formats, and giving students practice in making quick decisions and finishing a product in a given amount of time.

Writing to a Prompt during Standardized Assessment

First and foremost, all students should be apprised of the method of assessment that will be used to measure their achievement, and most states have chosen on-demand prompt writing as a means of assessing student achievement in writing. Not all states follow the same prompt format, the same time allowance, or the same assessment rubric, but a student's ability to write is measured by his ability to address the prompt thoroughly in a specific amount of time.

Becoming Familiar with the Prompt Format

Making sure your students know your state's prompt format is critical. This allows students to use the time allowed in meaningful ways, rather than reading the fine print, weighing their options, and going into the writing assessment feeling fragmented, unfamiliar with the task, and anxious.

Understanding the Necessary Structure

In the hundreds of student writing samples this author has read across the country, those that pass seem to have a certain structure. While identifying that structure as "the five paragraph essay" seems limiting, these essays really do look like the five paragraph essay: introduction, body, and conclusion. It is therefore important that students learn to address each question in the prompt in the body of their paper. If there are no questions in the prompt, students must become proficient in generating their own.

Realizing that Length Does Matter

Most states have a certain expectation of length. It revolves more around the student's ability to show "evidence of mastery" than it does an actual number of words or lines. Nevertheless, students need to be told that they should always strive to write more than one page.

Using Imagination

It doesn't always occur to students that they can make up the facts in a writing sample. One of the biggest problems students have in making a connection is that they haven't had the life experiences necessary to pull from memories about which that they want to write. As teachers, we must constantly remind students that they can make up their response. Most of the time, the prompt will remind you to *"write a real or make-believe story about . . ."* but students will still ask, *"Does it have to be true?"*

Making Decisions

Decision making is not easy for everyone, and one of the first things you have to do in prompt writing is to decide about which things you want to write! As a teacher, you may be thinking, *"But the prompt tells them what to write about!"* That may or may not be true. Consider these prompt scenarios.

My Best Friend, My Favorite Season, The Longest Day, If I Won the Lottery, and *When I Grow Up* all revolve around making a decision before the writer can begin to plan a story or essay.

In short, you can look at prompt writing one of two ways: as an unnatural means to an end in standardized assessment OR as an opportunity to let your students shine as they organize, analyze, discuss, reflect, respond, and take leadership roles in the classroom.

Chapter 3   Prompts . . . and More Prompts

Getting Ideas for Effective Prompts

Prompt Writing within the Literary Genre

Connecting Writing to Higher Level Thinking

Following Your State's Prompt Format

Prompts with Questions
Prompt Attack
Grades 3 and 4
Grades 5 and 6

Prompts without Questions
Grades 3 and 4
Grades 5 and 6

Prompts Based on Themes
Grades 3-6

Writing Every Day in the Classroom

The Simple 6 ™

Chapter 3: Prompts . . . and More Prompts

Getting Ideas for Effective Prompts

Where can I get ideas for effective prompts?

Ideas can be words, titles, or fully-written prompts. If you struggle with generating ideas for prompts, it's always helpful to brainstorm with a group of your colleagues. (Be sure to invite the creative minds!!) Once you get started brainstorming a list of ideas you'll piggyback on one another, and soon you'll have a collection of prompts from which to choose. The only rule you might want to keep in mind as you generate your list is this: Is the topic something my kids know and care about? That usually leads to three questions. What are we reading? What are we studying about in the content areas? What's happening in our world?

Rule 1: Ask your students to write about things they know about and are interested in.

What are we reading?
What are we studying?
What's happening in our world?

What are we reading?

Literature so often gives students the knowledge base they lack in real life, and that knowledge base is strengthened through fiction just as much as nonfiction. Writing about reading is only limited by the imagination. Why then, do so many teachers feel that they must assign the book report – based on literal comprehension and summarization? From the simple picture book to the multi-chapter novel, teachers can help students find connections to write about that will lead them into higher-level thinking and reflection.

What are we studying about in the content areas?

Whether it happens to be plants in science, the Boston Tea Party in social studies, Pablo Picasso's Blue Period in art, or the rules of a game in physical education, there are plenty of opportunities to write. Words of wisdom: If there is a worksheet for it, then there is also a writing topic to replace that worksheet. Don't think of writing as an added burden to an already loaded curriculum. Build knowledge in the content areas, and then bring writing to your lessons.

What's happening in our world?

There is a tendency to think of current events in two ways: the events that are happening today in real life and the events that typically happen yearly on any given date.

Obviously, events that are happening today are the kinds of writing topics that may come about spontaneously. Because you didn't know they were going to happen, they aren't really "planned for" in your weekly planner. World news, political events, weather-related tragedies, human interest stories, discoveries, inventions, economic trends, and local news are all catalysts for spontaneous writing. Keep an open mind and a flexible schedule when they do occur.

Yearly celebrations, or holidays, are the framework for instruction in many lower primary classrooms. Each month, students learn about the history or background for a particular celebration, which brings opportunities for writing and various art experiences. The major holidays alone give students at least 20 writing opportunities throughout the year.

Prompt Writing within the Literary Genre

There are four basic types of writing, if you're organizing by genre. They are narrative writing (personal and imaginative), expository writing, descriptive writing, and persuasive writing. Following are general ideas from each genre. Always tie them to what you are teaching.

NARRATIVE WRITING, or story writing, has all the elements of fiction – characters, setting, a central idea or problem, vivid descriptions of character interaction, and finally a conclusion or solution to the problem. Narrative writing can be personal or imaginative.

Personal
Tell a story about . . .

- being helpful
- being scared
- being embarrassed
- something funny that happened
- the worst day of your life
- stealing
- cheating
- being mean
- being nice
- being proud
- finishing first
- being the best
- winning
- losing
- playing a game
- sports
- weather
- a special place
- a vacation
- a special weekend
- a surprise visitor
- your relatives
- a holiday get together
- having a good friend
- getting along
- death
- loneliness
- feeling left out

Imaginative
Make up a story about . . .

- doing your best
- most boring day
- The Crazy Substitute Teacher
- The Day Our Teacher Turned into a Statue
- The Day the Teachers Stayed Home
- The Unbelievable Find
- Gone!
- Vanished!
- Lost!
- The Day I Was President
- The Day I Was Principal
- The Day I Ran the Candy Shop
- The Day I Invented the Homework Machine
- The Day I Won the Lottery
- The Day I Lost my Memory
- The Worst Storm
- The Best Trip
- The Unbelievable Gift
- I Finally Got What I Deserved
- The Winner Is . . .
- Payback
- Life Isn't Always Fair
- I Can Do It!
- No Way!
- If Only I Had. . .
- If I Were a Bird

EXPOSITORY WRITING explains or gives information. This type of writing requires thought and planning because the order of facts or events is important. Students might be giving directions, explaining the steps of a process, telling about a memorable event, or reporting information about something in which they are interested.

How to . . .   **Your Ideas:**

- ☐ clean your room
- ☐ send a package
- ☐ choose a pet
- ☐ plan a vacation
- ☐ stay out of trouble
- ☐ solve a math problem
- ☐ make a birthday card
- ☐ get ready for school
- ☐ find the best book
- ☐ choose a friend
- ☐ get information from the Internet
- ☐ be a good neighbor
- ☐ make spaghetti
- ☐ order a pizza
- ☐ pack for a camping trip
- ☐ make your bed
- ☐ make popcorn
- ☐ put a puzzle together
- ☐ play an outdoor game
- ☐ care for a pet
- ☐ be an A student
- ☐ make the best sandwich
- ☐ play a board game
- ☐ get along with people
- ☐ "charm" your parents into anything avoid bullies

DESCRIPTIVE WRITING paints a vivid picture of what is in the writer's mind and is interwoven throughout the other genres. In narrative writing, description plays an important role in clearly showing what is going on in the story – event by event. In expository writing description is used to relay information clearly. In persuasive writing powerful, descriptive language supports the writer's opinion and conveys passionate feelings about the topic.

Your Ideas:

- ☐ your school
- ☐ your teacher
- ☐ your classroom
- ☐ your favorite subject
- ☐ your family's car
- ☐ your favorite snack
- ☐ your mom's cooking
- ☐ something challenging
- ☐ something fun
- ☐ a sibling
- ☐ your family
- ☐ your house
- ☐ your idea of relaxation
- ☐ your favorite person
- ☐ an amazing sight
- ☐ your ambitions
- ☐ your likes
- ☐ your dislikes
- ☐ something you fear
- ☐ riding on an amusement park ride
- ☐ what makes you mad
- ☐ what makes you sad
- ☐ what makes you happy
- ☐ your interests
- ☐ the perfect vacation spot
- ☐ your room
- ☐ your talents
- ☐ your strengths
- ☐ your weaknesses
- ☐ your personality

PERSUASIVE WRITING gives students an opportunity to try to convince the audience to agree with their points of view. While persuasive writing is based on opinion, it must be supported with facts and examples. Logical thinking and inference are strong qualities of persuasive writing, and students must consider their audience when choosing the tone for the pieces.

Your Ideas:

- [ ] No More Book Reports
- [ ] Longer Lunch
- [ ] New Cafeteria
- [ ] More Before and After School Activities
- [ ] New Playground Equipment
- [ ] Less Homework
- [ ] Football for Girls
- [ ] New City Park
- [ ] Vote for Me
- [ ] More Enrichment Classes
- [ ] Good Grades Really Matter
- [ ] No Money for Music and Art
- [ ] I Need a Raise in my Allowance
- [ ] A Family Vacation
- [ ] Field Day Agenda
- [ ] Student Council Projects
- [ ] Metal Detectors at the Doors
- [ ] Fundraiser Dilemma
- [ ] Cell Phone in School
- [ ] Get Recess Back
- [ ] Old Enough to be Home Alone
- [ ] No Girls Allowed in Football
- [ ] Pets in School
- [ ] Don't Bully
- [ ] Don't Smoke
- [ ] Don't Drink
- [ ] Don't Take Drugs
- [ ] School Uniforms

Connecting Writing to Higher Level Thinking

Using Bloom's Taxonomy to organize your ideas is yet another way to make sure you are differentiating instruction to meet the needs of all students in your classroom.

Knowledge: Remember it.

At the knowledge level, students recall previously learned information. Writing tasks will ask students to define, describe, or recall.

Writing Ideas at the Knowledge Level . . .
What is an eagle?
How is a president elected?
Which state has the highest population?
Who was the fifth president?
What are the five major categories of vertebrates?

Comprehension: Interpret it!

At the comprehension level, students interpret literal meaning. Writing tasks will encourage students to explain, summarize, and interpret.

Writing Ideas at the Comprehension Level . . .
What is the main idea of this story?
What does this cartoon portray?
Summarize last night's presidential speech.
Based on the data in this table, what would you generalize?
What is the writer trying to say in this poem?

Application: Use it!

At the application level, students apply what they already know to new situations. Writing tasks will ask students to predict, solve, or transfer learning to a new situation.

Writing Ideas at the Application Level . . .
How will you teach this math concept to a friend?
Why do you think this is a good idea?
What reasons support your conclusion?
Why did you choose this answer?
What would happen if we skipped lunch every day this week?

Analysis: Take it apart!

At the analysis level, students break down situations or quantities of information into smaller, understandable parts. Writing tasks will encourage students to classify, analyze, and infer.

Writing Ideas at the Analysis Level . . .

What do you read between the lines?
What can you infer from this observation?
What is the best way to organize this task?
What information contributed to your being able to solve this mystery?
What was the author's purpose for writing this chapter?

Synthesis: Create it!

At the synthesis level, ideas are rearranged to form a new whole, clearly unlike what was there before. Writing tasks will ask students to hypothesize, modify, and create.

Writing Ideas at the Synthesis Level . . .

What would happen if. . .
Rewrite this story to make it more descriptive.
Write a mystery combining the characters from these two books.
Design a tool that will make this job easier. Write a description about that tool.
How many ways can you think of to solve this problem? Write about them.

Evaluation: Judge it!

At the evaluation level, students are asked to judge something based on a distinct set of criteria. Writing tasks will require students to defend, evaluate, and judge.

Writing Ideas at the Evaluation Level . . .

Why is this painting more valuable than others are?
If your house were on fire, which objects would you save?
Is this story well written?
Which one is the best?
Why doesn't this answer make sense?
Write a letter to the editor explaining your opinion.

Following Your State's Prompt Format

Getting ideas for prompts will get you started, but realize that it's important to follow the format your state uses. Seeing prompts in the assessment format makes students more familiar with what will be expected and diminishes anxiety. Across the United States, formats appear to fall into one of three categories: Prompts with questions, prompts without questions, and prompts based on a theme or general idea.

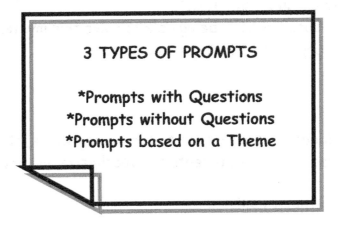

3 TYPES OF PROMPTS

*Prompts with Questions
*Prompts without Questions
*Prompts based on a Theme

Prompts with Questions

In terms of guiding structure, these are the easiest. If students have been taught to analyze a prompt and use the information rather than be intimidated by it, it clearly tells the writer what is expected to be included in the essay.

The prompt format is usually: a scenario or situation
questions that guide the writing content
the instructions
a rephrasing of the questions
reminders or restatement of the task

There are basically two types of
prompts
with questions:
The 3-Question Prompt
The What-Why Prompt

Name _____Grade _____

Teacher _____Date _____

3 Question Prompt: What I Learned in Third Grade

Read the information in the box. Then complete the writing activity.

The school year is almost over, and it's time to think back about what you learned this year. In which subject did you learn the most? What did you learn about behavior, such as good manners or being responsible? What else did you learn this year?

Write a letter to your teacher that describes what you learned this year. Be sure to include the subject in which you learned the most and what you learned about behavior in third grade. If you learned something else, tell about that also. Include as many details as you can to make your story interesting.

Pre-Writing Activity

Plan your writing on another sheet of paper before you begin your story.
Here are some questions to help with your writing:
    In which subject did you learn the most?
    What did you learn about behavior?
    What else did you learn?
Be sure your story has a beginning, a middle, and an end.
Include as many details as you can to make your writing interesting.

Your writing will be scored on how clearly you write and how well you get your ideas across. Be sure to check everything over before you turn it in.

PROMPT ATTACK!

Follow these steps to attack a 3-Question Prompt.

Step 1   Start with the title.

Step 2   Web the first question.
Write it as you would if you were asking yourself.

Step 3   Answer the question in a complete sentence.

Step 4   Add IDEAS for details.
If you can't think of any, leave blank *** to guide you in the number of sentences you will need in this part of your story.

Step 5   Repeat for the other questions.

Step 6   Use the strategies you know for writing an introduction.
Possibilities: Start with a hook. (might be a question)
    Develop a setting.
    Restate the title or topic.
(Lower level or younger writers might only restate the title.)

Step 7   Use the strategies you know for writing a conclusion.
Possibilities: Lead In – Include a transition sentences that leads into the conclusion.
Solve the problem or tell how the situation ends.
Finish with your feelings, an opinion, or some questions about which you still wonder.

Step 8   After about 10-15 minutes, you're ready to start your rough draft.

© Kay Davidson

3Q

Hook

Setting

Title/Topic

*

Q:
A:

*

Q:
A:

Q:
A:

*

Lead In

Solution

Thoughts

*

3Q

Hook
Setting
Title/Topic

I learned a lot in third grade.
*

Q: In which subject did I learn the most?
A: I learned the most in math
*

(oval) What I learned in third grade

Q: What else did I learn?
A: I learned all about art.
* Drawing
* Painting
* Planning space

Q: What did I learn about behavior?
A: I learned that it is important to have good manners.
* Please, thank you, excuse me
* kindness to others
* When the teacher talks I listen.

Lead In
Solution
Thoughts

I will miss third grade.
*

Student Response: Without the Prompt Attack

Dear Mrs. Davidson,

    I liked third grade this year because you are so nice and fun. But the best part is when you let us play games. This year I learned a lot of skills like to take your time, pay attition, and last of all lisen. My favorit subject this year was math because I learned a lot of things like how to multiply, dived and how to do a lot of stuff. I learned a lot of creavity skills like how to use my inageintion and how to write great stories then I learned how to paint great. But I wish it would never end.

Your student, Kayla

Student Response: With the Prompt Attack

Dear Mrs. Davidson,

I am so sad that this year is over. I am going to miss this class very much, but I want you to know that I learned A LOT in third grade.

My favorite subject was math. Math is my faverit because I am good at it. I mostly get good grades on it. I liked the math meeting, the math homework, and the math time tests.

I tryed to behave in class, but sometimes I got a little out of hand. I learned how important it is to have good manners. I always say please, thank you, and excuse me. I learned that if you don't say thank you, you will get your Bingo prize taken away. I tried to be kind to others. I learned that when the teacher is talking, I should lisen.

I learned so much about art. I think I will be an artist. I got a painting in the art gallery in the cafeteria. You told me it was a master piece. Best one in fact. I'm glad we got to paint so much this year.

That is what I learned in third grade. Do you think we will learn this much in fourth grade?

Your student, Cadi

Name _____ Grade _____

Teacher _____ Date _____

What-Why Prompt: MY FAVORITE SUBJECT

Read the information in the box. Then complete the writing activity.

Each day we learn things in many different subjects. It's only natural that you might like certain subjects more than others. What is your favorite subject? Why do you like it so much?

Write a letter to your teacher telling her which subject you like best. In your letter, include several reasons for your choice. You might like that subject because you're good at it, because you like the way it is taught, or because it challenges you to do your best thinking. You might just like it because you think it is fun!

Pre-Writing Activity

Plan your writing on another sheet of paper before you begin.
Here are some questions to help with your letter:
    What is your favorite subject?
    Why did you choose it?
Be sure your letter has a beginning, a middle, and an end.
Include as many details as you can to make your writing interesting.

Your writing will be scored on how clearly you write and how well you get your ideas across. Be sure to check everything over before you turn it in.

PROMPT ATTACK!

Follow these steps to attack a What/Why Prompt.

Step 1   Start with the title.

Step 2   Answer the What question.
            Write it as you would if you were asking yourself.
            The answer will most likely become part of your introduction.

Step 3   Add other IDEAS for your introduction.
            If you can't think of any, leave blank *** to guide you in the number of
            sentences you will need in this part of your story.

Step 4   Web Why #1 as its own paragraph.

Step 5   Repeat for Why #2 and Why #3.
            Consider using some of the ideas from the prompt for reasons.

Step 6   Use the strategies you know for writing an introduction.
            Possibilities: Start with a hook. (might be a question)
            Develop a setting OR
            write an overview of the reasons you are going to give.
            Restate the title or topic.
            (Lower level or younger writers might only restate the title.)

Step 7   Use the strategies you know for writing a conclusion.
            Possibilities: Lead into the ending.
                    Review your reasons.
                    Finish with your feelings, an opinion, or some questions
                    that you still wonder about.

Step 8   After about 10-15 minutes, you're ready to start your rough draft.

© Kay Davidson

Hook

Overview

Title/Topic

*

Why #1:
A:
*

Why #2:

A:

*

Why #3:
A:
*

Lead In

Overview

Thoughts

*

WW

Do you like math? I do! — Hook

timed tests, math meeting, math HW — Overview

That's why math is my favorite subject. — Title/Topic

*

Why #1: timed tests

A: Timed tests are fun.

*

My Favorite Subject

math meeting — Why #2:

A: We had a math meeting almost every day.

* teacher
* recorder

I've told you all about why I like math. — Lead In

timed tests, meeting, HW — Overview

* Is math your favorite subject? — Thoughts

Why #3: math HW

A: I really did like the math homework four nights a week.

* easy, fun
* parents check it

Student Response: Without the Prompt Attack

Dear Mrs. Davidson,

My favorite subject was math. I LOVED Saxon Math. We did it every day. I learned how to write a check. I learned how to do fractions. I learned how to do math meeting and I learned multiplication. It was so fun. We did side A at school and side B at home. I really like math. I am good at it too.

> Your math student,
> Tyler

Student Response: With the prompt attack

Dear Mrs. Davidson,

Do you like math? I do! I like math so much because of the timed tests, the math meeting, and the math homework. That's why math is my favorite subject.

Timed tests are fun. We got to race to see who could do the multication the fastest. We had three minutes for 100 problems. I got them all done every week!

We had a math meeting almost every day, but not Friday. If you were picked for the teacher, you got to call on people. If you got to be the recorder, you asked the questions out of the notebook.

I really did like the math homework. It was only four nights a week. It was easy and fun. We always did Side A first at school. Then our parence checked Side B at home. It was easy to get an A.

I've told you all about why I like math. The reasons were the timed tests, the math meeting, and the homework. Is math your favorite subject?

> Your favorite math student,
> Logan

Twenty Prompts with Questions for Grades 3 and 4

The following writing tasks are examples of the type of prompts you might find on a standardized writing assessment. These are designed to be transferred to a transparency and used throughout the year with your class.

My New Friend

You have just found a new friend, and you have so much in common! Your friend lives just a few houses away, and you will be able to do things together every day.

Who is your new friend?
How did you meet?
Why is this person so special?

Write a real or imaginary story that tells about your new friend. Be sure your story has a beginning, a middle, and an end. Write as many descriptive details as you can to make your story interesting.

The $50 Gift

It's an ordinary Friday, and the school day has almost ended. Suddenly your teacher says she has a surprise for everyone. On the way out the door, she hands each student a $50 bill.

Why would she do this?
What will you do with the money?
On Monday, how will you feel about your choice?

Write a real or imaginary story that tells about your $50 gift. Be sure your story has a beginning, a middle, and an end. Write as many descriptive details as you can to make your story interesting.

The Most Fun I Ever Had

The students in your class are sharing stories about the fun times during their lives.
What did you do?
Where did you go?
Who was with you?

Write a story that tells about a time when you had fun. Be sure your story has a beginning, a middle, and an end. Write as many descriptive details as you can to make your story interesting.

The New Pet

You have been bugging your mom for months about getting a pet. She has just told you that you may have a pet, but you will have to be responsible for taking care of it.

What pet will you choose?
Where will you get it?
How much work will it be to take care of this pet?

Write a real or make believe story that tells about your pet. Be sure your story has a beginning, a middle, and an end. Write as many descriptive details as you can to make your story interesting.

The Lunch Money

First thing this morning, you noticed that the girl who sits next to you left a $5 bill on top of her desk. As your class gets ready for lunch, she discovers that her money is gone.

What happened to the money?
How will you help her solve this problem?
What will you say to her if she doesn't find it?

Write a real or make believe story about the missing lunch money. Be sure your story has a beginning, a middle, and an end. Write as many descriptive details as you can to make your story interesting.

The Rainy Recess

You've been waiting all day for recess, and when you look outside you see it has started to rain. What happens in your school when it rains during recess?

What will you do?
Where will you go?
Who will be with you?

Write a story about what you do on a rainy recess day. Be sure your story has a beginning, a middle, and an end. Write as many descriptive details as you can to make your story interesting.

The Best Pizza in the World

Pizza is your favorite food in the whole world. You would eat it every day if you could. Describe the best pizza you have ever tasted.

Where did your pizza come from?   What was on your pizza?   Why did you like it?

Write a story that describes your favorite pizza. Be sure your story has a beginning, a middle, and an end. Write as many descriptive details as you can to make your pizza seem real.

How to Make a Bed

Your mom has just come into your bedroom and decided you need to clean it up. She tells you to start by making your bed.

Have you ever made your bed?
How do you do it?
What does it look like after you're finished?

Write a story that tells how you make your bed. Be sure your story has a beginning, a middle, and an end. Write as many descriptive details as you can so your explanation is clear.

A Special Guest

A special guest has been invited to your school, and you have been chosen by your teacher to give the guest a tour.

Who is the special guest?
What would you show the guest?
What kinds of things would you talk about?

Write a story about the visit. Tell who the visitor is and where you would take that person. Tell what you would see and what you would tell the visitor.

How to Pack the Best Lunch

You never like the school lunch, so your mom has agreed to let you make your own lunch twice a week.

What will you put in your lunch?
How will you pack it?
What will your friends say?

Write a story about the best lunch. Be sure your story has a beginning, a middle, and an end. Write as many descriptive details as you can to make your story interesting.

My Favorite Place

Everyone has a special place. It may be some place close by or a place you have visited that is far away. Tell about your favorite place and the reasons why you feel that way.

Where is your favorite place?   Why is it so special?
How do you feel when you have to leave?

Write a story about your favorite place. Be sure your story has a beginning, a middle, and an end. Write as many descriptive details as you can to make your story interesting.

Let me Show You

Grandparents can teach us a lot, but there are things you know how to do that your grandparents don't!

What are your grandparents like?
What can you teach your grandparents?
How will they react?

Write a story that tells what you will teach your grandparents. Be sure your story has a beginning, a middle, and an end. Write as many descriptive details as you can to make your story interesting.

Lost!

Getting lost is sometimes scary, but it can also be an exciting adventure—especially after you've been found! Write a real or make believe story about a time that you were lost.

Who was with you?
Where were you?
How were you "found"?

Be sure your story has a beginning, a middle, and an end. Write as many descriptive details as you can to make your story interesting.

My Favorite Time of Year

In some parts of the country you can easily tell what season it is, because the weather changes. In other locations, though, the weather is pretty much the same.

What is the weather like in your town?
What is your favorite time of the year?
Why?

Write a story that tells about your favorite time of year. Be sure your story has a beginning, a middle, and an end. Write as many descriptive details as you can to make your story interesting.

There is Nobody Like. . .

Is there someone in your family that stands out from the rest? Describe that person.
What do they look like?
How do they act?
How do you feel about that person?

Write a story about someone in your family. Be sure your story has a beginning, a middle, and an end. Write as many descriptive details as you can to make your story interesting.

Introducing. . .

You have just been notified that you have won an essay contest! You wrote an essay about the TV personality you would like to meet.

Whom did you choose?

Why did you choose that person?

What will you do when you meet that person?

Copy your winning essay here!

Principal for a Day

You have a new principal in your school, and you're wondering what she will be like. Since you've been a student in your school for at least two years, you've decided to give her some advice.

What advice will you give the new principal?

Why?

Write a letter to your principal giving her some advice. Be sure your letter has an introduction, a body, and a closing. Write with details and feeling so your principal will want to meet you!

Community Award

You have been asked to be on a committee that will decide who is named Citizen of the Year in your community. There are many wonderful candidates, but you may only choose one.

Whom did you choose?

What qualities will your person have?

Why do you think this person should win?

Write a story about the person you would choose to be named Citizen of the Year. Be sure your story has a beginning, a middle, and an end. Write as many descriptive details as you can to make your story interesting.

Happy Birthday!

Your birthday has finally arrived! You feel very grown up and much more responsible than last year. Stop! Instead of your real age, imagine you are turning 100!

How do you feel?

What memories can you share?

What advice can you give others to lead a great life?

Write a real or imaginary story about your birthday. Be sure your story has a beginning, a middle, and an end. Write as many descriptive details as you can to make your story interesting.

Family Vacation

Your family has been planning a vacation all year, and it's finally time to go!

Where will you go?

What will you do there?

Why did you choose that place?

Write a real or imaginary story about a family vacation. Be sure your story has a beginning, a middle, and an end. Write as many descriptive details as you can to make your story interesting.

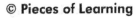

Twenty Prompts with Questions for Grades 5 and 6

That Cracks Me Up!
Your class is gathering funny stories that have happened in real life.

    What is the funniest thing you have ever seen?

    When did it happen?

    Why was it funny to you?

Write a real or make believe story about something you thought was funny. Be sure your story has a beginning, a middle, and an end. Write as many descriptive details as you can to make your story funny.

I Need an Allowance
Your parents have never believed in allowances. They have always felt that if you need money for something, you should just ask for it. Lately, though, when you ask they say, "No. We don't really think you need that."

    How will you convince your parents that you should have a weekly allowance?

    How much should they give you?

    What will you do to earn it?

Write a story about how you will convince your parents to give you an allowance. Be sure your story has a beginning, a middle, and an end. Write as many descriptive details as you can to make your story interesting.

Best Book
Your teacher makes you read a book each week outside of class. You thought it would be AWFUL, but you've actually found some books you really like.

    Which book if your favorite so far?

    Briefly, what is it about?

    Why did you like it?

Write a story about the best you have recently read. Be sure your story has a beginning, a middle, and an end. Write as many descriptive details as you can to make your story interesting.

What Did You Say?

A new student has just arrived in your class, and he does not speak English.

> What is his name?
> Where is he from?
> What will you do to help him adjust to your school?

Write a story about this new student. Be sure your story has a beginning, a middle, and an end. Write as many descriptive details as you can to make your story interesting.

Twin Day

Your principal just announced that this Friday will be Twin Day!

> Whom will you choose to be your twin?
> How will you plan to look alike?
> What will you do together during the school day?

Write a story that tells all about Twin Day! Be sure your story has a beginning, a middle, and an end. Write as many descriptive details as you can to make your story interesting.

The Dilemma

Your teacher has explained that a dilemma is a problem. Your class has a dilemma that you have been asked to solve.

> What is the dilemma?
> What suggestions will you give to solve it?
> Why do you think they will work?

Write a story about solving this dilemma. Be sure your story has a beginning, a middle, and an end. Write as many descriptive details as you can to make your story interesting.

No Electricity

A damaging storm ripped through your town last night, and the electricity has gone out. School has been canceled and many businesses are closed. What will you do today?

Write a real or imaginative essay about your day without electricity. What did you do? Who was with you? How did having no electricity affect you? Be sure to include many details to tell what your day was like.

Save the Environment

The Conservation Club in your school is sponsoring a Save the Environment contest. They have decided that the theme for this year will be Keeping Neighborhoods Clean and Safe. Can you think of an idea to help your neighborhood? How can your friends get involved? How will your city benefit?

Write an essay that explains an idea for how students your age can help keep your neighborhood clean and safe. What is your idea? How will students be involved? How will your city benefit from this idea?

Suddenly Rich!

A strange thing happened when you went to the mailbox this morning. You never get much mail, but today there was a small, brown box addressed to you. The return address was unreadable. When you opened the box, you found ten $100 bills inside! Where do you think it came from? What will you do with this money? What did you base your decision on?

Write a real or imaginary story about the day you found ten $100 bills in your mailbox. Be sure to include where you think it came from, what you will do with it, and how you made that decision.

My Collection

Many students your age like to collect things. Girls sometimes collect dolls, boys may collect baseball cards, and kids in general just like to collect "stuff". Do you have a collection? If so, what do you collect? If not, what would you like to collect? Why would you choose to collect this?

Write an essay describing a collection you have or would like to have. Tell why you chose your collection and why you think collecting something would be fun and interesting.

Trading Places

Rather than "Take your Son or Daughter to Work Day", your school has decided to ask students to think about trading places with Mom or Dad for a day. Which parent do you choose to trade places with? Why? What do you think their day is like?

Write an essay about trading places with your mom or dad. What do you think their day is like? Be sure to include as many details as you can to make your essay interesting.

That was Close!

From time to time, we find ourselves in situations that are dangerous. Disasters, accidents, being in the wrong place at the wrong time, or just using poor judgment might put you in a tight spot. In what situation did you find yourself? Did you escape the situation on your own, or did someone else help you? How did everything turn out?

Write a real or imaginary story about a time you had a close call in a dangerous situation. Tell all about what happened, how you escaped, and how everything turned out in the end.

Day Off!!

It's an ordinary Wednesday, and the radio has announced that a power line came down near your school and it will be closed. Your parents have already left for work. What will you do?

Write a real or imaginary story about the day school was closed and your parents had already left for the day. Include many descriptive details to tell about your day. Be sure to include whom you called, what you did all day, and how you felt about it.

I Want to Be Just Like _____

A role model is someone you look up to because that person has set good examples for others to follow. Who is your role model? What is this person like? What kinds of things can you do to be more like this person?

Write an essay telling all about your role model. Be sure to include what this person is like, why you respect them, and how you can be more like them.

Please Don't Touch That!

You're in a store and you spy something extremely interesting. Even though the sign says not to, you reach your hand out to touch it. Just as your fingers approach the object, the store manager yells, "Please! Don't touch that!!" As he yells, he startles you and causes your hand to fly into the object. Where are you? What is the object? What happens next?

Write a real or imaginary story about a time you were in a store and touched something you weren't supposed to. In detail, tell where you were, what the object was, and what happened.

No More Recess!!

Because test scores have dropped, school administrators have decided that students in the upper grades will no longer have recess. The members of the student council are urging students to write a letter to the principal convincing him that this will not help solve the problem.

Write a letter to your principal telling him why you think recess should be kept in the schedule. Give specific reasons to support your opinion.

Survival of the Fittest

Over the years, animals have learned to adapt to their environments in order to survive. Think of an animal that lives in a particular habitat. What three characteristics of this animal help it to survive?

Write an essay in which you describe this animal. Include the characteristics this animal has that help it survive in its habitat.

I Spy . . . a Triangle!

Geometric shapes are everywhere! You just have to look for them. Think of three shapes. Tell where these shapes might be found and how they are used in everyday life.

Write a descriptive story about shapes. Tell what shapes you see, where you see them, and how they might be used. Include several descriptive details in your story.

Let's Talk About It

There is something you have wanting to talk to your parents about, but you don't really know if you can or you can't. What is the subject? Why is it so hard to approach them? What are you going to do about it?

Write a letter to your parents telling them about this subject about which you want to talk to them. You might mention why you think it is so hard to approach them, and set up a time when you can all sit down and talk.

Dear Diary

Everyone in your class is going to keep a diary for one week. You do not have to be yourself. You can pretend to be anyone you choose! Whom will you choose to be? What will you write about? In what time era will you choose to live?

Write the first entry in your diary. Be sure to tell who you are, where you are, and many details about the day – including your feelings! Don't forget the date.

Prompts without Questions

Prompts without questions are used most often on standardized assessment. Many students feel that this is the easiest type of prompt to write to, because a concrete idea is given, but there are no parameters. This gives students an opportunity to be much more creative than they might have been had the questions been provided.

The downfall, however, is that while students may prefer this type of prompt, their writing usually lacks structure and paragraph development. In order to organize their thoughts, students must come up with their own questions – using those to organize the paragraphs of the body.

> *The prompt format is usually:*
>
> *a scenario or situation*
>
> *an idea of what you might want to write about*

After School Fun

Read the information in the box. Then complete the writing activity.

Your parents decided that you will go to the after-school program until they can pick you up after work. Tell what the after school program is like or what you think would make it better.

Pre-Writing Activity

Ideas you have about this topic:

Choose 3. Turn them into questions.

Question 1:

Question 2:

Question 3:

Your writing will be scored on how clearly you write and how well you get your ideas across. Be sure to check everything over before you turn it in.

PROMPT ATTACK!

Follow these steps to attack a prompt without questions . . .
The biggest difference between attacking prompts with questions and prompts without questions is obvious. If questions aren't given, students need to generate their own. These will be the basis for the paragraphs in the body.

Step 1   Start with the scenario that is given. How much do you know about this topic?

Step 2   Take a minute or two to jot down as many ideas as you can about this topic. Turn three of those ideas into questions that you will answer in your story or essay.

Step 3   Web the first question.
Write it as you would if you were asking yourself.
Place it very close to the introduction, because the answer may become part of your introduction.

Step 4   Answer the question in a complete sentence.

Step 5   Add IDEAS for details.
If you can't think of any, leave blank *** to guide you in the number of sentences you will need in this part of your story.

Step 6   Web Why #1 as its own paragraph.
Repeat for Why #2 and Why #3.
Consider using some of the ideas from the prompt for reasons.

Step 7   Use the strategies you know for writing an introduction.
Possibilities: Start with a hook. (might be a question)
Develop a setting OR
write an overview of the reasons you are going to give.
Restate the title or topic.
(Lower level or younger writers might only restate the title.)

Step 8   Use the strategies you know for writing a conclusion.
Possibilities: Lead into the ending.
Review your reasons.
Finish with your feelings, an opinion, or some questions that you still wonder about.

Step 9   After about 10-15 minutes, you're ready to start your rough draft.

3Q

Hook

Setting

Title/Topic

*

Q:
A:

*

Q:
A:

Lead In

Solution

Thoughts

Q:
A:

*

Q:
A:

*

*

Hook

Setting

Title/Topic

Lead In

Solution

Thoughts

3Q

Have you ever been in an after school program?

You wouldn't want to.

The after school program is not fun. It is boring.

Q: What kinds of things do we do?
A: We do whatever we want.

* homework
* running around
* games

After School Fun

Q: What is the teacher like?
A: The teacher is really bad.

* no control
*doesn't help with HW

Q: How could it be better?
A: Anything would be better
than this.
* more games
* better teacher
* control the kids

It is terrible!

Solve it by getting me out of here.

* Can't I stay home alone?

After-School Fun: Without the Prompt Attack

We are in an after school program that is very fun! We get to play games, run after everyone, and play tag, and play checkers. If you want you can do your homework at the cafeteria tables. Sometimes people will bother you but you can tell them to go away. We can bring snacks and leave the mess. I think the teacher will clean it up. The teacher is nice. He is pretty quiet so the kids run around a lot. The regular teachers would not like it. They would want the kids to be quiet.

After-School: With the Prompt Attack

Have you ever been in an after-school program? You wouldn't want to. The after-school program is not fun. it is boring and awful.

We do whatever we want in the after-school program. You can do homework, but it is loud in there and you can never think. You can play games but everyone is arguing and fighting. Some of the pieces are missing. Mostly people run around.

The teacher is a moron. He lets everybody run around. It is very stressful because he can't control the kids. He also doesn't help with homework.

Anything would be better than this. If we had better games with all the pieces, and if we had a better teacher who could control the kids it would be OK. Snacks would be good too. We never had those.

The after-school program is terrible!!!! We need to solve this by getting me out of here. I hate it, especially at the end of the day. Can't I stay home alone?

Twenty Prompts without Questions for Grades 3 and 4

I Remember

Everyone has memories. Recall your favorite memory, and write a descriptive story about it.

I'm Running Away!

Write a real or make believe story about a time you were so mad you told your parents you were going to run away.

Three Wishes

You have been given three wishes. Tell how you will use them.

The Unexpected Gift

Imagine that you could give a gift to anyone of your choice for no reason. Write a story about giving an unexpected gift to someone.

I Didn't Mean to Do It!

Sooner or later everyone is involved in a situation where something happened "by accident". Write a story about something that happened to you.

The Desk Drawer

There is a drawer in the teacher's desk that is always locked. Write a story about what you think is in the draw.

My Favorite Relative

Write a descriptive story about your favorite relative.

Time Out!

Write a real or imaginary story about something that happened to send you to the Time Out chair!

It's Not Dark Out!

Write about what it feels like to have parents who make you go to bed at 8:00, when all your friends are still out and about.

My Mom

Write a descriptive story about your mom.

Just an Ordinary Day

Write about an ordinary day – either a weekday or a weekend day. Tell about the kinds of things you do.

The Most Memorable Fund Raiser

Your class thought it was a great idea to earn for the Homeless Shelter in your town. Everyone decided that having a car wash was the best idea. The day of the car wash, however, everything went wrong!

Quiet Time

Your teacher says it's a good idea for everyone to have 30 minutes of quiet time every day. Tell how you choose to spend this time each day.

Earliest Memory

Search back into your memory and tell about the earliest thing you can remember

The Best Gift

Tell about the best gift you ever received.

The Dog Didn't Eat my Homework . . .

but here's what really happened to it. Write an imaginary story about the day you did not bring your homework to school.

My Favorite Game

Your teacher is buying games for the class and wants your opinion.

The Unusual Backpack

As you came into school this morning, you saw a backpack just outside the door. Suddenly, you noticed that it was moving. Tell about what was inside the backpack and what you decided to do with it.

You're Staying After School!

It's definitely not your day. Everything has gone wrong, and now you have to write a letter to your parents telling about the trouble you had at school.

Game Rules

Think of your favorite game. Using specific details explain how to play it.

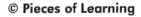

Twenty Prompts without Questions for Grades 5 and 6

My Least Favorite Relative

Write a descriptive story about your least favorite relative.

"Do as I say, and not as I do," is an old, famous saying. What does this mean?

My Dad

Write an essay telling what your dad is like or what you'd like him to be like.

That's not True!

Write about something that you used to think was true but you know now is not.

The Worst Storm Ever

Write a real or imaginary story about the time you were caught in a storm.

Just Like _____

Write a story about a role model that has been important in your life.

One Day Trip

Describe a place you have always wanted to visit.

Designer Bedroom

If you could have any kind of bedroom, what would yours be like?

I Take it Back!

Tell about a time something happened that you wish you could take back.

The Big Event

Convince your parents to take you to the big event of your choice.

The Shopping Trip

Describe the best shopping trip ever.

Sports

Sports sometimes play a huge role in how we spend our leisure time. Tell about how sports affect your life.

Time line-Life Event

Think back over the years since you were born. Tell about an event that you clearly remember.

Unique

Everyone is unique in some way. Tell how you are different or unique from everyone else.

Special Birthday Party

You've just been given $100 to spend on your own special birthday party. Tell about what you have in mind and how you will spend the money.

My Name

People are named for many different reasons, and sometimes for no reason at all! Write a real or imaginary story of how you got your name.

Favorite Holiday

Tell about your favorite holiday and why it is special to you.

Worst Fear

Most people have something they are afraid of. Write a story about your worst fear and some ways of how you might get over it.

My Town

The places we live in come in all sizes and types. Tell what living in your town is like.

Change is Good

If you could change one thing about yourself, what would it be?

Prompts Based on a Theme or General Idea

States that use this type of prompt usually give more than one option for the essay, letting students choose their genre. While choice is good, especially in writing, students are faced with the first dilemma – which one to pick; and too much time is spent on choosing rather than on writing. Students must now decide how they will address the idea or theme, generate their own questions, and set up some type of graphic organizer to guide the structure of their piece.

The prompt format is usually: a word or theme
a statement that lets you choose how you would address this topic
several one-sentence ideas from which to choose

46 Theme-Based Prompts for Grades 3 to 6

Theme: Accomplishment

Think of something you have accomplished that was difficult. Write a story about this activity or event.

Theme: Adolescence

With adolescence comes added pressure and responsibility. How are you handling it?

Theme: Aging

How does aging change people?

Theme: Accidents

Are people accident prone, or do they really just have accidents on purpose?

Theme: Anger

Tell about a time you wish you had controlled your anger.

Theme: Bravery

Write a real or make believe story where you or someone you know showed bravery.

Theme: Change

If you could change one thing about yourself, what would it be?

Theme: Commitment

What does commitment mean to you?

Theme: Conflict

Conflict comes in many forms. Describe what it means to you.

Theme: Criticism

When is criticism a good thing?

Theme: Death

Reflect on your feelings about death.

Theme: Decisions

Write an essay about a time you made a poor decision and regretted it later.

Theme: Differences

Everyone is different. How is this a good thing?

Theme: Discovery

Many important inventions have changed people's lives. Discuss the invention you think has made the biggest change in the way people live.

Theme: Effort

Tell about why it's always important to put forth your best effort.

Theme: Embarrassment

Everyone has embarrassing moments. Write about one of yours.

Theme: Experience

They say, "Experience is the best teacher". What does this mean to you?

Theme: Fairness

Write a story about a time you thought you were treated unfairly.

Theme: Friendship

Write about a real or make believe time when you did something outstanding or memorable for a friend.

Theme: Friendship

You and your friend made plans a long time ago to spend this evening together playing. Now, because of the weather, you must play inside.

Theme: Friendship

Write a letter to your friend describing a game that you would like to play. Explain why this is the best game for two people to play indoors.

Theme: Frustration

Write a real or imaginary story about a time you tried to learn something that wasn't very easy for you.

Theme: Honesty

Tell about a time when you did something that showed you were an honest (or dishonest) person.

Theme: Honor

What does the honor in honor roll mean?

Theme: Humiliation

Have you ever been humiliated? Describe the situation.

Theme: Imagination

If you could be any animal, what would it be and what would your life be like

Theme: Imagination

Imagine that last night while you were sleeping you shrunk. You are now only 18 inches tall.

Theme: Imagination

Imagine that you are asked to keep a chimpanzee for a week. Write a story about your unusual experiences with the chimpanzee.

Theme: Individuality

Why is individuality important to you? How do you express it?

~~~~~~

Theme: Kindness

Explain how small acts of kindness can change the world.

Theme: Life

What's the best advice you could give for how people should live their lives.

~~~~~~

Theme: Love

What is love?

~~~~~~

Theme: Memories

Think back to a moment you'll never forget. Write about what happened and why you will always remember it.

~~~~~~

Theme: Peace

Is it possible to have world peace?

~~~~~~

Theme: Peer Pressure

Write a story about a time you gave in to peer pressure or stood up to your friends and said NO.

~~~~~~

Theme: Praise

Why is praise so important, no matter how old you are?

~~~~~~

Theme: Respect

Explain how to get others to respect you.

~~~~~~

Theme: Responsibility

Write a story about a time when you showed that you were a responsible person.

Theme: Service/Helping

Think of someone in your neighborhood you might be able to help.

Theme: Superstition

Do you believe in superstition? Tell why or why not.

Theme: Technology

How has the computer changed your life?

Theme: Tradition

Think of a tradition your family has. It may or may not be tied to a holiday.

Theme: Truth

Explain why you think it is always best to tell the truth.

Theme: Understanding

Tell about something that you have trouble understanding.

Theme: Uniqueness

How are you unique?

Theme: Wealth

Wealth is very important to some people. Write a real or imaginative story

Writing Every Day in the Classroom

If you were asked to list 10 different ways that your students write each week, could you? Here are opportunities that can keep students engaged in writing every week of the school year.

- *Vocabulary definitions* . . . help students to be specific in their descriptions (rather than always saying, it's like . . .)

- *Spelling sentences* . . . help students master skills in sentence structure and word usage.

- *Free writes* . . . encourage students to spontaneously brainstorm, writing down whatever comes to mind.

- *Literature responses* . . . give students practice in thinking and responding at higher levels.

- *Letter/note writing* . . . gives students an opportunity to talk about their thoughts.

- *Book reviews* . . . allow students to practice skills in concise summarization, and encourage them to focus on descriptive language or an overall opinion.

- *Science lab observations* . . . are perfect opportunities to encourage students to ask questions, develop hypotheses, and reflect.

- *Social studies simulations* . . . give students an opportunity to recap historical events as if they were there.

- *Social studies event overviews* . . . enable teachers to check for understanding as well as writing skills.

- *Nonfiction, fact-based writing* . . . gives students practice in recognizing main idea vs. details as well as sharpening skills in paraphrasing and organizing.

- *Problem solving in social situations* . . . encourages students to think at higher levels and consider multiple viewpoints.

- *Articulating mathematical thinking* . . . is something we all need to do more often.

- *Fine arts reflections* . . . help students perfect skills at the evaluation level of Bloom's Taxonomy.

- *Prompt writing* . . . lets the writer see the task from two viewpoints: as the student writing the prompt and the student writing *about* the prompt.

There are many opportunities for writing in the classroom. Teachers typically say, *"I've got so many standards to teach, there isn't time for writing."* Actually, the reverse is true. The overwhelming pressure that teachers feel to "teach the standards" should be the catalyst for change. Abandon worksheet assignments. Limit isolated cognitive skill lessons. Learn to integrate throughout the curriculum. If you start thinking in terms of units, themes, or "big ideas," you will find that you are teaching students, not standards. Here is a checklist that will give you some ideas for organizing your standards by theme or "big idea." By starting with a content area (science or social studies) and integrating from there, you will be able to say honestly that you've covered all the standards for your grade level without having to check them off every week.

1. Plan in advance (during the summer).
    Identify science and social studies topics and organize them by their standards.
    Create units of study and chart them on a content unit map for the entire year.
    Integrate basal stories or novel studies with your content themes.

2. Once the literature titles are established and mapped, integrate all the language arts requirements.
    Match required spelling lists with the appropriate literature or content, or make up your own spelling-vocabulary list.
    Create higher-level questions that will generate reflective rather than literal responses.
    Make a list of the mechanics skills that are expected to be introduced and/or mastered during the year. Analysis of student writing and charting skill deficiencies will tell you on which skill to focus in your weekly grammar mini lesson.

3. Plan out each quarter so you can see the bigger picture.
    Have a binder for each quarter to help organization.
    Include a weekly overview page for quickly scanning the week's activities.
    If you are using any worksheets, limit them to five for the week.
    Put master copies of them in this binder, and run them off at one time.

4. Build a weekly structure in your plan book – and stick to it.

5. Celebrate with Fun Week!

When students write every day, they become aware of the multitude of types of writing. It's about variety, and it's about making school fun. If school is fun, students are motivated. If students are motivated, they try harder. When students try harder, they learn more. That learning comes from your expertise and willingness to integrate curriculum, offer individual encouragement, manage time, plan mini lessons, analyze data, and allow students to take charge of their own writing as they work with peers to revise and edit.

© Pieces of Learning

Chapter 4: Simplifying Formal Writing Assessment in the Classroom

Assessment Across the District

The Assessment Packet

Scoring Tips

Scoring (mini rubric) x 4

Student Writing Samples and Anchor Papers

Converting a Rubric Score to a Grade Book Score

Using Data to Drive Instruction

The Simple 6 ™

Chapter 4   Simplifying Formal Writing Assessment
in the Classroom

All writing is not assessed or brought to publication. However, there are times when assessment is necessary – or reporting student progress on a report card as well as for school improvement documentation.

Assessment Across the District

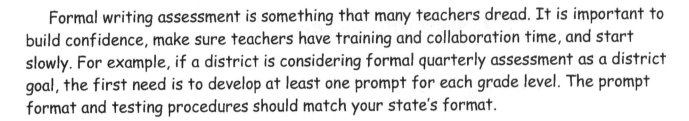

Formal writing assessment is something that many teachers dread. It is important to build confidence, make sure teachers have training and collaboration time, and start slowly. For example, if a district is considering formal quarterly assessment as a district goal, the first need is to develop at least one prompt for each grade level. The prompt format and testing procedures should match your state's format.

If teachers are reminded at the beginning of the assessment month, they can integrate writing as they design lesson plans. Have students complete the writing two to three weeks prior to the end of the month so teachers can use the scores as part of their quarterly classroom assessment as well. Allow a one-week window for giving the prompt, and allow another week's window for scoring the prompt. Score all papers with a mini rubric, and transfer all scores to a *Class Analysis Sheet* (page 155) and turn in by the Friday of the scoring week.

The school administrator or writing chair can then compile data. Analysis of all school data should be shared with staff members by the following Friday. This reporting of data falls into the same category as homework. If you don't have time to grade it and promptly return it, don't assign it. By the same token, if teachers are being asked to assign and grade within a specific time frame, they should be entitled to data analysis in a timely fashion as well. It's takes little time at a staff meeting to update everyone regarding progress on building goals. Do it.

In large districts, this information should then be transferred from building administrator to central office. All schools are then charted and compared. A brief analysis should be included, as well as plans for intervention.

Time Table

Week 1: Students write from the same prompt at each grade level. Use assessment packet on the following pages for district-wide quarterly assessment.

Week 2: Teachers score the writing samples and complete the Class Analysis Chart. A copy of the chart is due in the school office by Friday.

Week 3: Administrators compile and analyze the data, reporting to teachers by Friday. A copy of the data analysis is due in the central office by Friday.

Week 4: The Central office administrator compiles data from each school. Analysis (and plans for intervention) are returned to each school by Friday.

Student _____

Teacher _____

Date _____

Assessment Packet

Grades 2-6

SCORE ___/6

___/4

Title

Read the information in the box. Then complete the writing activity.

Prompt scenario. Questions.

Directions. Repeat the questions in sentence format.

Pre-Writing Activity

Plan your writing on other paper before you begin.

Be sure your story has a beginning, a middle, and an end.

Here are some questions to help you organize your story.

    *

    *

    *

Add details to make your writing interesting.

Write on as many lines as possible. The length of your story should be more than one page.

_____

_____

_____

_____

_____

_____

_____

_____

_____

_____

_____

_____

_____

_____

_____

_____

_____

_____

_____

_____

_____

_____

_____

Your writing will be scored on how well you write and how well you get your ideas across. Be sure to check everything over before you turn your story in.

Proofreading Checklist

1. Have you started each sentence with a capital letter?
2. Have you capitalized names of people and places?
3. Have you ended each sentence with the correct punctuation mark?
4. Have you spelled all words correctly?
5. Does the subject of your sentence agree with the action word? (verb)
6. Have you written complete sentences?

The Simple 6 ™ A Writing Rubric for Kids

Ask these questions:
0 / 1

____ **STICK TO THE TOPIC:**   Did you **stick to the topic**, or did you run away with some other idea?

____ **LOGICAL ORDER:**   Have you presented your thoughts in a **logical order** that included an inviting beginning and a strong conclusion?

____ **INTERESTING WORDS:**   Have you overused generic vocabulary, or have you gone back to look for opportunities to use **interesting words?**

____ **DIFFERENT SENTENCE PATTERNS:**   Have you tried to create interest and variety by using **different sentence patterns?**

____ **DESCRIPTIVE SENTENCES:**   Did you write **descriptive sentences** that made the reader aware of his senses?

____ **AUDIENCE:**   Did you write for a specific **audience**? Were you original, lively, or authoritative?

© Kay Davidson, 2004

____ / 6   TOTAL POINTS

LANGUAGE CONVENTIONS RUBRIC

☐ SCORE 4 VERY GOOD	☐ SCORE 3 ADEQUATE	☐ SCORE 2 MINIMAL	☐ SCORE 1 POOR
• There are few or no errors in: capitalization punctuation subj./verb agreement complete sentences spelling	• There are some errors in: capitalization punctuation subj./verb agreement complete sentences spelling	• There are many errors in: capitalization punctuation subj./verb agreement complete sentences spelling	• There are many serious errors in: capitalization punctuation subj./verb agreement complete sentences spelling

Assessment in the Classroom

How often?

Assessment for instructional purposes will probably happen more often than local assessment for a school improvement plan. Schedule it, and stick to it. An appropriate assessment is four times each (nine-week grading) period possibly weeks 2, 4, 6, and 8.

What's the procedure?

Assign a writing topic or prompt idea that closely resembles your state format. Don't forget to relate writing topics to what you are studying.

Procedure A: Thursday/Friday Format

During weeks 2, 4, and 6, go back to the Thursday/Friday format that was used during implementation. Use data from your Class Analysis Sheet to design the lessons. On Thursday, motivate students or teach a lesson, introduce the prompt, and have students write up to the rough draft. Let the piece rest over night. Prior to Friday, read over the rough drafts, reteach a general weakness to the entire class, and allow students to work in small groups for revision and editing. (You would pull flexible groups at this time.) Students would then recopy final drafts and turn them in on Friday.

Procedure B: Testing Simulation

"Rehearse" a testing situation during week 8. Give the prompt with the exact directions and time limit that would be given during a state assessment on Thursday. Prior to Friday, all papers need to be scored. Fill out a Class Analysis Sheet. Spend Friday writing time reviewing general weaknesses with the entire class and possibly showing examples. Then have students read, discuss, revise, and edit in small groups.

Scoring Tips

The best way to improve your scoring skills is to dive right in and start scoring student writing. Use a mini rubric, provided in Appendix A. The more you practice, the better and faster you will be. In the beginning, you might consider meeting with a few colleagues to score together. Put your students' papers in a folder, and exchange them with a colleague. Each person in the group then reads the first paper orally, scores it, and "thinks out loud," justifying each point. If not everyone agrees, discuss differences of opinion or expectations. After everyone in the group has taken a turn reading the first paper and explaining scoring thoughts, each teacher can then proceed to score the rest of the papers in the folder. If you come across a paper that you are unsure of, separate it from the pile, and discuss it as a group at the end.

Words of Advice about Scoring

Set aside a block of time (less than an hour) in which you will score all papers.
Gather mini rubrics and a Class Analysis Chart.
Score each paper, one at a time – without dwelling for long periods of time making decisions.

Suggested Procedures:
Read it first. Assign the score based on only the components done well.
OR: Decide if you think it is passing or not. Then Simple 6™ it.

If you know it will not pass:
Decide which 3 components or less will get points.
Score 3 papers usually have length but many problems within.
Score 2 papers are short, weak attempts at completing the task. Many times these papers will be hard to read because of spelling and punctuation errors.
Score 1 papers are any attempt at the task – even less than one sentence.
Note attempted on the rubric for very weak papers.

If you know it is going to pass:
The stakes for each point get higher as you move toward the Score 6.
In *sticking to the topic*, most prompt questions should be addressed.
   How well did the writer accomplish the task?
Logical order **must** include a beginning, a middle, and an end.
   Is the piece introduced with an inviting beginning or topic sentence?
   Does it naturally flow as you read?
   Are transitions smooth?
   Is there a definite conclusion?

Vocabulary should be precise and/or above grade level.

    Have words specific to the subject been used?

    Do any words stand out as being above grade level?

    Were the exceptional vocabulary words used correctly?

If *different sentence patterns* were used, did they contribute to the fluency of the writing?

    Has the writer avoided making the piece sound like a list?

    Are questions and exclamations used to make an impact?

    Do you see evidence of complex and/or compound sentences?

There should be many *details* and *descriptions*.

    Just how descriptive is the piece?

    How many examples were given?

    Did the writer appeal to your senses?

    Were proper nouns used?

    Was a strong attempt made to create a visual image?

The writer should have definitely connected with the *audience.*

Do thought shots, enthusiasm, compassion, humor, or personal style pull you into the writing?

Tips by Grade Level:

Grade 3: Remember, third grade is part of the real deal in many states, meaning that these students are formally assessed on a state standardized test. Be careful not to be too lenient on points, because you will instill false security. Look at the overall piece. Decide, by its logic and length of content, if you think it will pass. If you know it won't, you have to decide which points to award – not to exceed 3. Very weak pieces usually get 1-2 points for attempts.

Grade 4: Writing should be focused and organized with smooth transitions. There should be a definite feeling of beginning, middle, and end. Explanations and examples should be detailed. An attempt at improving the level of vocabulary should be noticeable.

Grade 5: Writing should come from an organized framework that shows planning and forethought. Topic sentences should identify each paragraph. Paragraphs should be developed by using detailed descriptions and examples that reinforce the topic sentence.

Grade 6: Remember, you may now be required to use the secondary rubric and expectations. Planning and prewriting are essential. Questions within the prompt must be addressed. Details must support each topic sentence. Sentences should be more complex, and transitions should be smooth. You should start to see evidence of literary devices that promote a personal connection with the audience.

Anchor Papers

The following pages provide mini rubrics and prompts and anchor papers at each grade level. A completed mini rubric and detailed description of the points will guide you as you learn to score student writing samples with the Simple 6™.

The Simple 6 ™

0 / 1

____ Stick to the Topic
____ Logical Order
____ Interesting Words
____ Different Sentence Patterns
____ Descriptive Sentences
____ Audience
____ TOTAL POINTS

©Kay Davidson, Revised 2002

The Simple 6 ™

0 / 1

____ Stick to the Topic
____ Logical Order
____ Interesting Words
____ Different Sentence Patterns
____ Descriptive Sentences
____ Audience
____ TOTAL POINTS

©Kay Davidson, Revised 2002

The Simple 6 ™

0 / 1

____ Stick to the Topic
____ Logical Order
____ Interesting Words
____ Different Sentence Patterns
____ Descriptive Sentences
____ Audience
____ TOTAL POINTS

©Kay Davidson, Revised 2002

The Simple 6 ™

0 / 1

____ Stick to the Topic
____ Logical Order
____ Interesting Words
____ Different Sentence Patterns
____ Descriptive Sentences
____ Audience
____ TOTAL POINTS

©Kay Davidson, Revised 2002

Name _____   Grade 3

Teacher/School _____

Date _____   SCORE ___ / 6

___ / 4

The New Pet

Read the information in the box. Then complete the writing activity.

You have been bugging your mom for months about getting a pet. She has just told you that you may have a pet, but you will have to be responsible for taking care of it. Describe the pet you will choose. Where will you get it? How much work will it be to take care of this pet?

Write a real or make-believe story about your new pet. Be sure to include a description of your pet, where you will get it, and the kinds of things you will do to help take care of your pet.

Pre-Writing Activity

Plan your writing on other paper before you begin.
Be sure your story has a beginning, a middle, and an end.

Here are some questions to help you organize your story.
   What pet will you choose?
   Where will you get it?
   How much work will it be to take care of this pet?

Add details to make your writing interesting.
Write on as many lines as possible. The length of your story should be more than one page.

Your writing will be scored on how clearly you write and how well you get your ideas across. Be sure to check over everything before you turn it in.

monkey I will ge if it make from the zoo to have as my one bet folevery. I will have a red and blacy monkey for my pet name.

The Simple 6 ™

0 / 1
<u>att 1</u> Stick to the Topic
_____ Logical Order
_____ Interesting Words
_____ Different Sentence Patterns
_____ Descriptive Sentences
_____ Audience

1   TOTAL POINTS

Assessment Commentary:
A Score 1 paper is short. It is hard to make sense of it as you are reading. This paper, which seems to include the title in the text, is hard to follow. The student has attempted to stick to the topic because we see the word pet. The scorer must infer that the monkey will come from the zoo and that it will be black and white, so no point attempt is given for descriptive sentences.

I will get a green Lizrd. it will be from the petshop. and it wil only tak me in the afternoon. To take care of it. and I will fede him his best food.

The Simple 6 ™

0 / 1

__1__ Stick to the Topic
____ Logical Order
____ Interesting Words
____ Different Sentence Patterns
____ Descriptive Sentences
____ Audience

1 TOTAL POINTS

Assessment Commentary:
This Score 1 paper is higher than the first sample. We don't see the word pet but we know it will be a green lizard. A second attempt point for descriptive sentences was not given because the sample does not make sense. For a low-functioning student who is struggling to get this much content, some teachers may award the second point for attempting descriptive sentences.

If I got a pet I would get a bichan and Name it sammy and play with him every second of the day we would play fetch and teach him how to sit and keep him forever!

The Simple 6 ™

0 / 1

<u>att 1</u>   Stick to the Topic
_____   Logical Order
_____   Interesting Words
_____   Different Sentence Patterns
<u>att 1</u>   Descriptive Sentences
_____   Audience

2   TOTAL POINTS

Assessment Commentary:
A Score 2 paper is longer than a Score 1 and makes more sense. The student receives points for attempting to master tasks within the rubric. This student attempts sticking to the topic because we see the word pet. Even though we don't know what the pet is, attempts were made to include details.

Do you want to know about my new pet? I will have a pet dog it is a small dog. It is a rock-raller. I buy it at a pet stor. My dog's name is Nick. I will give it water and dog food. I will tran my dog a lot.

The Simple 6 ™

0 / 1

__1__   Stick to the Topic

_____   Logical Order

_____   Interesting Words

_____   Different Sentence Patterns

att _1_   Descriptive Sentences

_____   Audience

2   TOTAL POINTS

Assessment Commentary:
This Score 2 is higher than the first. The sentences are longer and easier to understand, including the hook at the beginning. Points are given for Stick to the Topic and attempting to include Descriptive Sentences. If the final sentence had been, "That's how I will take care of my pet," this sample would have also gotten the point for Logical Order and would have been a Score 3.

New Pet

Mom finally let me get a pet now. I told her it was going to be a big Horse. It's a she. I got her from a fantastic farmer and his terrific wife. there were lots of adoring animals but I could only have one! I was getting a funny, black with some wight, and is cute, horse. She does lots of tricks. I bought her and brung her home. I found out what to feed her. She gets lots of room. I give her tender, love, and care. I clean up the messes and groom her. The messes stink I clean her too. I named her Little Jeenie. It's hard taking care of animals. Horses are cute. Don't you think so?

The Simple 6 ™

0 / 1
__1__ Stick to the Topic
_____ Logical Order
__1__ Interesting Words
_____ Different Sentence Patterns
__1__ Descriptive Sentences
_____ Audience

3   TOTAL POINTS

Assessment Commentary:
This sample gets points for Stick to the Topic, Interesting Words, and Descriptive Sentences. She focuses on the task, even though the story is fragmented and has no real order. Interesting Words (challenging vocabulary) were: fantastic, terrific, adoring, and groom. While she touches on connecting with the audience, the point was given for Descriptive Sentences because of the number of examples that were given.

My Baby Kitten

My mom just told me that I could get any kind of animal I want. But I have to take caer of it myself. So I been decided to get a cat named Alicia. She was at Sam's Pet store. You would love it.

The Simple 6 ™

0 / 1
___1___ Stick to the Topic
___1___ Logical Order
_____ Interesting Words
_____ Different Sentence Patterns
att 1 Descriptive Sentences
_____ Audience

3 TOTAL POINTS

Assessment Commentary:
This is a typical Score 3 paper. It gets points for Stick to the Topic, Logical Order, and an attempt at Descriptive Sentences. What does Alicia the cat look like? What happened the day you went to Sam's Pet Store? How will you take care of the cat? More details in each of these areas would increase the length of the piece. With encouragement, this writer could also add more comments to connect with the reader, bringing it closer to the Score 4.

My New Pet

I have been thinking about getting a cuddly and furry pet. Do you know what it is? It's a ginni pig! I want the littlest ginni pig in the universe! "Mom can I go to that hewmunges pet shop?" blabbered Kattie in a very loud voice. "I guess". yelled Katie's mom. When I got there I was so excited! The very small guy showed me the ginnie pigs. I asked him if he had one smallest ginni pig. He said yes. He said it is a beautiful goldish brown and has blue eyes too. She is very, very friendly too. I took her gently home. I wanted him because I can always play with it and love it.

The Simple 6 ™

0 / 1
__1__ Stick to the Topic
__1__ Logical Order
_____ Interesting Words
_____ Different Sentence Patterns
__1__ Descriptive Sentences
__1__ Audience

4   TOTAL POINTS

Assessment Commentary:
This sample gets points for Stick to the Topic, Logical Order, Descriptive Sentences, and Audience. The story is obviously about getting a pet, and it is relatively easy to follow the order of her thinking. While she makes an attempt at using Interesting Words, the point wasn't given for universe and hewmunges. I questioned the usage of blabbered and yelled, and the other words used were more descriptive than challenging. While she had a great start on Different Sentence Patterns, the last half of the story fell into the subject-pronoun pattern. Remember: As soon as a paper gets to the Score 4 range (passing) no points are given for attempts.

The Pet I always wanted

I asked my mom a thousand times if we could have a baby panther. The thousand and one time she finally said, "yes". So we went to the zoo we asked the box how much do he want for a baby panther he said four thousand dollars. My mom said your going to work for that much money. When we got home I got straight to work I worked for 24 hours and seven days a week. When I had four thousand dollars we went to the zoo to buy the baby panther. When we got there the guide person opened the cage for us. The panther was all black and had red eyes. so I named him Brus. When we got him home I played with him. When my friends came over they are scared of Brus. So when my friends come over I will put h

im in a cage and every time he's hungry I'll give him food. That's the pet I always wanted.

The Simple 6 ™

0 / 1

_1_	Stick to the Topic
_1_	Logical Order
____	Interesting Words
_1_	Different Sentence Patterns
_1_	Descriptive Sentences
____	Audience

4 TOTAL POINTS

Assessment Commentary:
This is a lower level Score 4, getting points for Stick to the Topic, Logical Order, Different Sentence Patterns, and Descriptive Sentences. While we would like the order to flow a little better than it does and the descriptions to be more developed, it has enough evidence of mastery to be considered a passing paper.

My Pet! Not Yours!

Hi, I'm Lucy. I'm very excited because I've been begging my mom for months to let me get a pet, a Chihuahua to be exact and finally my wish has come true! Today she is taking me to a pet store called Paws of Pets. What kind of dorky name is that? Anyway it's time to go!

"Finally!" We just got here and I'm in HEAVEN! There are sooo many Chihuahuas I don't know which to choose! Finally I see the one I love. It has an off white color. It's very small and her name is Honeydue. The pet shop owner told me she is three weeks old. "I'm getting her!'

On the way home I got to hold her so she could get used to me. I'm also thinking about what my two year old brother is going to do to her.

Later that night I kept her in my room. "This is terrible! She isn't housetrained!" Let's just say she made a . . .mess! My mom said I should get a doggy door for her to go in and out of my room and that she would help me to housetrain her. That wasn't fun, but at least there were no more messes.

One day while I was at school Honeydue got out of my room because I forgot to lock the doggy door. To make it worse she went into my brothers room while he was sleeping and woke him up. My mom had a fit! Now if he gets out again I to am in big big trouble.

Now that Honeydue is five weeks old things have calmed down and Honeydue is happier and isn't waking my brother anymore (yes!). I am still keeping her in my room and taking good care of her and I think she will be my best pet for a long time!

The Simple 6 ™

0 / 1

___1___ Stick to the Topic

___1___ Logical Order

_____ Interesting Words

___1___ Different Sentence Patterns

___1___ Descriptive Sentences

___1___ Audience

5   TOTAL POINTS

Assessment Commentary:

The Audience connection is immediately apparent in this Score 5 paper. What is just as obviously missing? Interesting Words. She easily gets points for Stick to the Topic and Logical Order (which includes her inviting beginning and strong conclusion). Evidence of statements, questions, exclamations, dialogue, and the complexity of her sentences give her the point for Different Sentence Patterns. Again, while we might like to see more detail in the Descriptive Sentences, this is Grade 3.

My Mystery Pet

If I could choose a pet, do you know what animal I would choose? I will give you a hint in almost every sentence. If I got a pet I would get one with a pink nose. Do you have a guess on what it could be? Here's another hint. It can be black, white, brown, or these colors mixed. Now, any gesses? OK. More hints. It has big, floppy ears. Do you think you know what it is yet? Most dogs and cats attack them. Do you know now? It has a cotton ball like tail. My animal loves to hop. You can get my pet from Petsmart.

If you gessed a bunny you were right! I will play with it, feed it, and keep it safe. It will take a lot of kindness and love to take care of such a small animal but I know I can do it!

The Simple 6 ™

0 / 1

_1_	Stick to the Topic
_1_	Logical Order
___	Interesting Words
_1_	Different Sentence Patterns
_1_	Descriptive Sentences
_1_	Audience

4   TOTAL POINTS

Assessment Commentary:

For a Grade 3 student, this is a strong Score 5 paper – and a unique one at that. The connection with the audience is almost immediate, with a unique style that involves the reader in guessing. This student gets points for Stick to the Topic, Logical Order, Different Sentence Patterns, and Audience. While sentence patterns are relatively simple, she includes many different types that contribute to the overall fluency of the piece. Descriptive sentences could have included more details, but it's important to remember that this is a Grade 3 student. Interesting Words (Challenging Vocabulary) was the only point missing.

Student Sample A: Grade 3 Score 6

Did you know a mongoose is going to be a pet of mine? How I'm getting this creature is very simple. First I'm going to obtain a world map and then I'm going to pinpoint where they live. I would probably find it on the plains somewhere. Next, I'm going to get the things I'll need to capture it. It is facile, so I may not be able to catch it. If I can't I'll design a trap to catch him in. A mongoose is more than one foot tall so I'll need a net and probably a cage so I can bring him home. Finally I will have to capture it's parents so they won't be too worried. My mongoose family is going to be blue with orange stripes. They're going to need some food so I will have to find some snakes for them to eat, but that includes more work. It will be hard and maybe dangerous but I have earned a pet. And I perceive the danger, but it will be extremely hard for me to tame it. That includes trying to improve its conduct. If you try to do this you'll find yourself breathing like a maniac. So hard you might collapse. So now you know how hard it would be to have a mongoose for a pet. I know what to name it. It's going to be Lucky, because I'm going to take care of him and his family for the rest of there life. This will be the most recollectionable capture I would ever have!

The Simple 6 ™

0 / 1

1	Stick to the Topic
1	Logical Order
1	Interesting Words
1	Different Sentence Patterns
1	Descriptive Sentences
1	Audience
6	TOTAL POINTS

Assessment Commentary:
What an interesting Score 6 sample from a Grade 3 student! This boy obviously knows a lot about the mongoose species since he perceives the danger in having one. and he realizes they will be hard to catch because they are so facile. Obvious points in all components. Again, while we would have liked it to be in perfect order with developed paragraphs, this is a Grade 3 student.

Peewee

Hi! I'm Anibbelle. I've been bugging my mom to let me get a Bear Hamster. Anibbelle! We're ready for you presintashon! Okey, be down in a minet! I told my mom if I put on like a slide show about how I would take care of Peewee, (Bear Hamster) then she might aproove of him or her.

Anibbell! Hury up! I'm getting old! Hold your horse moma. I'm coming. Stom! Stomp (down stares). Presenting Anibbelle's slide show!

Da,da,da,da,da,daaaa! This is Peewee. He's a Bear Hamster. After school yesterday I went to the pet store. The store clurk let me hold a femail Hamster. He said "The femailes don't stink as mutch." "Because they go to the bath-room in the same spot. But mails stink more because they go to the bathroom all over the cage.

I'll feed him every day, change his cage once a week, and take him out of the cage every day so he'll keep tame. Sound like I'm responsible? Please, (down on knee's) please, please please! Okey. You can get, Peewee. I trust you'll do every thing you sed. Oh, I will, I will, I really will! When can I get him? I suposs we can get his cage tonight. Then you can get him tomarow after school. Don't forget to ask the man at the pet store what he eats.

When Anibelle was in school she thougt it would never end. When Mrs. Field called on Anibbelle for the answer of 5x10. Anibbelle replied Peewee, and the class lafed. When school was finly over Anibbleel was so anxshous that she darted straight to the pet shop. She was walking home with Peewee when the box started to vibrate. What are you doing Peewee? Mimmicking a chain saw? When they got home and Peewee was in the cage Anibbelle noticed a hole in the box. So you like to chew ha, said Anibbelle. I'll get some toys for you tomarow. and some food too. I was so excited today I forgot to ask what you eat.

When Anibbelle came home from school the next day Peewee was dead! Anibbelle fell to her knee's and burst into tears. She waled so hard you could have heard her on the other side of the work. Mama came in and looked at Peewee. She asked Anibbelle, did you feed Peewee yesterday? NO. I dident. I forgot to. Because Aynne asked me if I could play so I forgot to go to the pet store to get his food and a toy. Well Anibbelle, pets always come first said mama. let this be a lesson to you.

The Simple 6 ™

0 / 1

_1_	Stick to the Topic
_1_	Logical Order
_1_	Interesting Words
_1_	Different Sentence Patterns
_1_	Descriptive Sentences
_1_	Audience

6 TOTAL POINTS

Assessment Commentary:

The point for connecting with the Audience is the first one you encounter. This writer easily draws you into the scenario of her making a presentation to her mother so she can get a hamster. Words like presentation, responsible, clurk, anxshous, vibrate, and mimicking are recognized as Interesting Words, even though they are not spelled correctly. Despite this student's lack of mastery of the mechanics of dialogue, the story is easy to follow. It is sad ending comes as a surprise, and while we would have liked it to be more developed, this is Grade 3.

Name _____   Grade 4

Teacher/School _____

Date _____   SCORE ___ / 6

___ / 4

How to Pack the Best Lunch

Read the information in the box. Then complete the writing activity.

You never like the school lunch, so your mom has agreed to let you make your own twice a week. Your lunches are so noticeable, that the school newspaper has asked you to write an article in a series about "The Best Lunches." What do you usually put in your lunch? How do you pack it? Why is your lunch so great?

Write an article for the school newspaper that tells about your lunch and what is so noticeable. Be sure to include as many details as you can to make your article interesting.

Pre-Writing Activity

Plan your writing on other paper before you begin.
Be sure your story has a beginning, a middle, and an end.

Here are some questions to help you organize your story.
    What do you usually put in your lunch?
    How do you pack it?
    Why is your lunch so great?

Add details to make your writing interesting.
Write on as many lines as possible. The length of your story should be more than one page.

Your writing will be scored on how clearly you write and how well you get your ideas across. Be sure to check over everything before you turn it in.

I have meatball and egg sandwitches with a millon dollers in it.

The Simple 6 ™

0 / 1

___1___ Stick to the Topic

_____ Logical Order

_____ Interesting Words

_____ Different Sentence Patterns

_____ Descriptive Sentences

_____ Audience

1   TOTAL POINTS

Assessment Commentary:

This Score 1 Sticks to the Topic, even though we don't see mention of the word lunch. No point is given for attempted details because the few that are included don't contribute to connecting the writing to the topic.

Apple are my favite because is good for you.

The Simple 6 ™

0 / 1
att 1 Stick to the Topic
_____ Logical Order
_____ Interesting Words
_____ Different Sentence Patterns
_____ Descriptive Sentences
_____ Audience

1   TOTAL POINTS

Assessment Commentary:
One point is given for attempting to Stick to the Topic.

One day I was going to lunch. When I sat down I looked in I saw a heater. In the heater there was macroni and chees with snickers.

It was wonderful it was the best I would put the heater on one side and the snickers on the other. It was wonderful   The End

The Simple 6 ™

0 / 1

___1___ Stick to the Topic

_____ Logical Order

_____ Interesting Words

_____ Different Sentence Patterns

att 1 Descriptive Sentences

_____ Audience

2   TOTAL POINTS

Assessment Commentary:
This student sample Sticks to the Topic and attempts to give several Descriptive Sentences, even though they don't necessarily make sense.

I packed tomato soap, some chips, and a Subway sandwich. Whele I put the tomato soap in to a Cataner. I put
the chips into a little bages. Why is it so great the never
cook Subway sandwichs.

The Simple 6 ™

0 / 1

___1___ Stick to the Topic

_____ Logical Order

_____ Interesting Words

_____ Different Sentence Patterns

att 1 Descriptive Sentences

_____ Audience

2 TOTAL POINTS

Assessment Commentary:
Two points are given for Stick to the Topic and an attempt to include Descriptive
Sentences.

If I don't like the school's lunch and my mom agreed to let me pack twice a week I would choose to pack lemonade, pizza, fudge, and fruit snacks. It would be packed with a lunch box, containers for the fudge and the pizza, and I would also put ice packs in to keep everything cold. The reason why it would be great is because it tastes good and everything would be homemade except for the fruit snacks. That is how I would pack my lunch.

The Simple 6 ™

0 / 1
 _1_ Stick to the Topic
 _1_ Logical Order
 ___ Interesting Words
 ___ Different Sentence Patterns
 _1_ Descriptive Sentences
 ___ Audience

3   TOTAL POINTS

Assessment Commentary:
This is a typical Score 3 paper, although it's slightly on the short side. The sample Sticks to the Topic, has Logical Order, and includes some Descriptive Sentences.

My lunch is a meatball and bologna sandwhich and an orange juice. I put an Ice pack in first. Then the orange
juice. Finally the sandwhich. I put it all in my lunch box.
It is so great because you get to eat it. That is what I do
to pack my own lunch.

The Simple 6 ™

0 / 1
<u>1</u>   Stick to the Topic
<u>1</u>   Logical Order
<u> </u>   Interesting Words
<u> </u>   Different Sentence Patterns
<u>1</u>   Descriptive Sentences
<u> </u>   Audience

3   TOTAL POINTS

Assessment Commentary:
*This is a very low level Score 3, but it does include evidence of three components: Stick
to the Topic, Logical Order, and an attempt at Descriptive Sentences.*

The best lunches to pack for your school lunches. Well, I don't pack lunches vary often because I like what they make at school. For all of you who like packing here are some great ideas.

What I like to most is sub sandwitches. for exsample turkey, blogna, ham, or roast beef but you can have whatever you want. Don't forget the mayo!

Vetshable are good for you too. you can pack a salde with green leafy spinch, carrots, dressing, and sun flower seeds. You could pack peas, green beans, corn, solaflower, broccooil too. You can also put in some vetshable dip or some ranch dresing.

Fruits are delishous and good for you too. You can pack apples, peaches, pares, ornges, or grapes. That would be healthy for you.

You can't forget about your drinks. water, jucie, grape fruit juice is good for you too.

The Simple 6 ™

0 / 1
_1_	Stick to the Topic
_____	Logical Order
_____	Interesting Words
_____	Different Sentence Patterns
_1_	Descriptive Sentences
_1_	Audience

3   TOTAL POINTS

Assessment Commentary:
This Score 3 sample Sticks to the Topic but ends without a conclusion, so no point is given for Logical Order. There were no Interesting Words, and Sentence Patterns didn't always contribute to the fluency of the writing. Many examples were given for a point in Descriptive Sentences, and the conversational tone gives a point for Audience.

All the kids at my school think my packed lunches are super-duper. Everyone asks me "how did you do it?" Well, listen carefully because I'm going to tell you all my tips for an outstanding lunch. First, my mom buys cute little containers and sandwich bags with cool designs on them. My mom also buys Pringles with jokes on them, and the people who are sitting around me get to here them. I bring juice boxes that has sour stuff in the straw so whenever you drink your juice box you make funny faces and everyone watches you drink it. I bring desert nobody's ever seen before, like vanilla pudding with everyone's favorite fruit in it, like when our school has fruit festival day. My lunches are so unique and delicious, but they also entertain the people who sit at my table. Sometimes I even trade food or share with them, like tomorrow I will bring fortune cookies. So now you know exactly why everyone loves my packed lunches and why everyone wants to sit by me.

The Simple 6™

0 / 1

__1__ Stick to the Topic

__1__ Logical Order

_____ Interesting Words

__1__ Different Sentence Patterns

_____ Descriptive Sentences

__1__ Audience

4 TOTAL POINTS

Assessment Commentary:
This short story has the potential to be a Score 6 without too much revision. She definitely Sticks to the Topic, has Logical Order, Descriptive Sentences, and makes a connection to the Audience. Little effort would be needed to improve the quality of the vocabulary and to make Sentence Patterns contribute to the overall fluency of the piece.

The way you pack the best lunch is to put everything you want to pack in a container. That way nothing gets smashed. If I were you, I would pack a bulony, kechup, and cheese sandwich with a yogurt, banana, and a water, but pack what you want. When you get everything in a container put them in your lunch bag very neatly and organized. To keep your food cold you should put a freezer pack in the bottom of your lunch bag. If your food needs to be kept cold, and you don't have a freezer pack your food will spoil You won't be able to eat your food. After you get everything pack and neatly packed you can put it in your backpack or you can carry it. This the way to pack is better than just throwing your food in. This way your food is just as good to eat as when it's fresh from the groery store. I don't get why anyone would pack a lunch another way. Why would they want to pack their lunch another way? That's all I have to say. Have great lunch!

The **Simple 6** ™

0 / 1

1	Stick to the Topic
1	Logical Order
___	Interesting Words
___	Different Sentence Patterns
1	Descriptive Sentences
1	Audience

4 TOTAL POINTS

Assessment Commentary:
This Score 4, like the one before it, gets points for Stick to the Topic, Logical Order, Descriptive Sentences, and Audience. Revision strategies would include working on Sentence Patterns to make sentence transitions smoother and to beef up the Vocabulary.

This is how I got my lunch in the newspaper. From fruits and vetabals to candy and exsotic drinks, I always plan ahead. Most of the stuff I bring is really cool, like one time I brought a strawberry, kiwi, banna, and peach fruit punch. Everybody wanted to try it!

Rather than a sandwich, I prefer to bring wraps in my lunch with cheese and ham on a tortia shell. One of the vetebals I bring is a defat fried zucceenie. None of the stuff I bring is in fancy containers. It's mostly in plastic bags. And sometimes if I'm good my mom slips a peace of candy in my lunch. I always appreciate that, especially if it is chocolate. All this food when it comes to school, is in an attractive pink lunch box. That's how I got my lunch in the school newspaper. It's really not that hard if you plan ahead and bring cool stuff.

The Simple 6 ™

0 / 1

1	Stick to the Topic
1	Logical Order
1	Interesting Words
	Different Sentence Patterns
1	Descriptive Sentences
1	Audience

5   TOTAL POINTS

Assessment Commentary:
This sample is relatively simple and to the point. It gets a Score 5 for Sticking to the Topic, having Logical Order, Interesting Words, Descriptive Sentences, and Audience. Using different Sentence Patterns to create smoother transitions would easily bring this paper to a Score 6, even though it is relatively short.

This is how I like to pack my lunch. I like to eat a ham sandwitch on wheat bread with mustard. I also have a bag of washed grapes, an orange, chesse and chrackers, and a bottle of water. First, I like to put a ice pack in the bottem of my container so that food stayes cold. Next, put the sandwitch in a plastick bag so it dose not get soggy.

Then wash the grapes in the sink, but don't use soap. They won't taste good if you do. Fourth but not final, you put the bottle of water in next to the ice pack so it stays cold. Finally put the chrackers and chesse in a bag and put it in. I like to keep it on top so the chrackers don't get smashed.

I think my lunch is the best because it is colorful and healthy. It's also easy to do, and the food isn't really anything that special. Just follow my instructions. And then, well, enjoy.

The **Simple 6** ™

0 / 1

__1__ Stick to the Topic
__1__ Logical Order
_____ Interesting Words
__1__ Different Sentence Patterns
__1__ Descriptive Sentences
__1__ Audience

5 TOTAL POINTS

Assessment Commentary:
This Score 5 sample Sticks to the Topic, has Logical Order, Different Sentence Patterns that contribute to the fluency of the piece, Descriptive Sentences, and connects with the Audience. Revision for Interesting Words would help this piece, and additional details would have made this a higher Score 5.

The Best Lunch

If you want to pack a great lunch, listen to this. First, get a colorful lunchbox, just to cheer up your day. Next, pick what kind of food you want. There are so many things to choose from! There's salty stuff, fruit, and other nutritional snacks, and of course, a sandwich. There's a lot of stuff you can do to not just have an ordinary lunch. Here is how to do it.

First, you can pick any kind of sandwich you want. Ham and cheese is always good, but then so is peanut butter and jelly. After you make your sandwich you take a cookie cutter and pick a shape. It could be a star, a heart, anything. Once you pick one you can make your sandwich into that shape! Using this idea also eliminates the crusts if you don't like them.

Another easy tip is to get a colorful napkin or something. My mom goes to the store after a holiday and gets them on sale. Then she uses them the next year. If you are making lunch for someone else, enclose a note inside. I love it when my mom does that! It cheers me up sometimes when I'm not in a good mood.

Make sure to pick out just the right beverage. Of course you can always get milk at school, white or chocolate. Some people prefer water, but I always bring a cold fruit drink. And don't forget to put it in with an ice pack.

Well, those are my tips. Enjoy your lunch!

The Simple 6™

0 / 1

1	Stick to the Topic
1	Logical Order
1	Interesting Words
1	Different Sentence Patterns
1	Descriptive Sentences
1	Audience

6   TOTAL POINTS

Assessment Commentary:
This piece gets a point in every category. If I had to make any kind of suggestion, it would be to insert more challenging vocabulary words and to increase the length of the conclusion.

My Lunch

Everyone always thinks my lunches are the best, or at least the most unusual. Yesterday for my lunch I brought a meatball sandwich and steak. Everyone was looking at my sandwich and my lunchbox, because you could smell it everywhere in the cafeteria! They hadn't even seen the most amazing part yet. When I opened my lunchbox, there was a heater keeping my sandwich and my steak warm! On the other side of my lunchbox, there was a freezer compartment keeping my chocolate milkshake, my peanutbutter buddy bar, and my homemade raspberry pie cool.

The teachers were so amazed they called a newspaper writer to interview me about my lunch, and especially about my lunchbox. I told them how my dad was an ingenious inventor who thought up the hot and cold lunchbox. I told them how it works and why I chose my lunch.

What a great day! Now, they're going to interview me about how I got to school too. Lucky for me, my dad invented a vehicle that runs on distilled water. It gets excellent gas mileage, but it looks very unusual. I can't wait to tell them all about that.

The Simple 6 ™

0 / 1

_1_	Stick to the Topic
_1_	Logical Order
_1_	Interesting Words
_1_	Different Sentence Patterns
_1_	Descriptive Sentences
_1_	Audience

6   TOTAL POINTS

Assessment Commentary:
This Score 6 has it all . . . but could always get better with more details.

The Longest Day of My Life!

Read the information in the box. Then complete the writing activity.

You have just returned home after a long day—the longest day of your life! You plop down in the chair, and your mom comes around the corner and says, "So, how was your day?"

What will you tell her? Be as descriptive as possible as you tell her what you did all day, whether or not anyone was with you, and why the day seemed so long.

Write a story that describes your day.

Pre-Writing Activity

Plan your writing on other paper before you begin.
Be sure your story has a beginning, a middle, and an end.

Here are some questions to help you organize your story.
    what you did all day
    whether or not anyone was with you
    why the day seemed so long
    descriptive details about how you feel

Add details to make your writing interesting.
Write on as many lines as possible. The length of your story should be more than one page.

Your writing will be scored on how clearly you write and how well you get your ideas across. Be sure to check everything over before you turn it in.

I came home after school to plop on my bed to think what I did in school.

The Simple 6 ™

0 / 1

_1_	Stick to the Topic
_____	Logical Order
_____	Interesting Words
_____	Different Sentence Patterns
_____	Descriptive Sentences
_____	Audience

1   TOTAL POINTS

Assessment Commentary:
This Score 1 paper gets one point for attempting to Stick to the Topic.

When I come home on a hot summer day. My mom ask me how my day was. I say it long.

The Simple 6 ™

0 / 1
att 1 Stick to the Topic
_____ Logical Order
_____ Interesting Words
_____ Different Sentence Patterns
_____ Descriptive Sentences
_____ Audience

1   TOTAL POINTS

Assessment Commentary:
This Score 1 paper gives a very brief overview of the assigned topic, with one point being given for attempting to Stick to the Topic.

My mom walks in my room and said how was your day. In the morning I had to read and do the practice book pages and then gym we ran 3 laps. I watch a movie and then walk home.

The Simple 6 ™

0 / 1

__1__	Stick to the Topic
_____	Logical Order
_____	Interesting Words
_____	Different Sentence Patterns
att 1	Descriptive Sentences
_____	Audience

2   TOTAL POINTS

Assessment Commentary:
This Score 2 Sticks to the Topic, although it does not address all the questions in the prompt. It provides some detailed information, but Descriptive Sentences are not developed to the fullest.

I came home with a back eye one day. The bully push me and my best friend and that was the longest day ever.

The Simple 6 ™

0 / 1
___1___ Stick to the Topic
_____ Logical Order
_____ Interesting Words
_____ Different Sentence Patterns
__att 1__ Descriptive Sentences
_____ Audience

2 TOTAL POINTS

Assessment Commentary:
This sample was given two points for Stick to the Topic and attempting Descriptive Sentences. Details need to be further developed.

An AWESOME Day!

Today me and my friends went shopping at the U.S.A.'s largest mall! After we did that we stopped to get some ice cream. Then when we got back to my house we went swimming at the pool. It was 95☐ F weather!

The only people that went were me and my friends.

The reason our day seemed so long was because the sun was shining so hot that it made our life actually a little bit miserable—but hey—at least we got a nice sun tan!

We are all very tired but we had a very cool day!

That was our AWESOME day!

The Simple 6 ™

0 / 1

__1__   Stick to the Topic
__1__   Logical Order
_____   Interesting Words
_____   Different Sentence Patterns
_____   Descriptive Sentences
att 1 Audience

3   TOTAL POINTS

Assessment Commentary:
This Score 3 paper gets points for Stick to the Topic, Logical Order, and attempting to connect with the Audience. Interesting Words are not challenging enough for Grade 5 and many more details are needed before a point would be given for Descriptive Sentences.

The Longest Day of My Life

"Oh Hi Joel How was your day," said mom and this is how it goes, nobody was with me ontil later. I was 11 years old and I was walking in the woods when all of a sudden. "OOOWW", something call. Then and there I saw him an Indain. I was shaking, scary and whatchful. Than the Indain said, "How are", I said, good" later, here we are I am trying to shoot a watermeolon with a bow and arrow at the third try I hit the watermealand. Now I showed the Indain how to shoot a gun. he hit the watermealand the first try. He was happy the day seemed long because we made each others laught. and Have Tuneadments the day not long but seemed long. Then He took me to his tribe. Then I went home smiling on that is what I did all day.

The **Simple 6** ™

0 / 1

___1___ Stick to the Topic
___1___ Logical Order
_____ Interesting Words
_____ Different Sentence Patterns
att 1 Descriptive Sentences
_____ Audience

3   TOTAL POINTS

Assessment Commentary:
In this Score 3 sample we see is a paper that seems to Stick to the but has details that are hard to follow. We will give the point for Logical Order because there is a beginning, middle, and end. There was also an attempt made to provide details in Descriptive Sentences, even though we might struggle to see the writer's vision. Sentence Patterns and spelling errors make it difficult to follow what's happening in the middle, even though a variety of types are used. Obviously, there is no evidence of Interesting Words or making a connection with the Audience.

A Day at the Smoky Mountains.

"Hi, Mom. I just wanted to let you know we were back in town. I'll be home in about five minutes. I can't wait to see you to tell you all about the trip!"

"Oh hi Honey. I just walked in the door and plopped down in my favorite chair. I'm so glad to hear your back. I can't wait to hear all about it! Maybe we can go out for a pizza and you can fill me in on all the details."

"Mom, I would love to, but I am absolutely exhausted! Today, before we left, Karen and I walked to the pool and raced each other for 20 laps. We hung out there until lunch so we could say good-bye to our friends. Then we biked up the mountain and looked down at the gorgeous valley below one last time while we ate our lunch. We biked back down the trail, met Karen's parents, and have been in the car ever since. It doesn't really seem like we did that much today, but it feels like this has been the longest day of my life! To top it off, the sun was beating down on us, and I've got some sunburn that's not feeling too great at the moment."

As the car pulled into our driveway, I thanked Karen and her parents. We had had so much fun, but it was such a looonnng fun day. I think my mom will soon see that I could sleep without dinner.

The Simple 6 ™

0 / 1
_1_	Stick to the Topic
_1_	Logical Order
___	Interesting Words
_1_	Different Sentence Patterns
_1_	Descriptive Sentences
___	Audience

4   TOTAL POINTS

Assessment Commentary:
This is an interesting Score 4 that took a slightly different twist from the prompt. The writer is not the one who plopped down in the chair after a long day. She is coming home from a trip, talking to her mom on a cell phone. The twist does not deter from the original prompt instructions, giving her a point for Stick to the Topic. The story has Logical Order but no Interesting Words. Sentence Patterns and Descriptive Sentences contribute to the Score 4.

The longest day Ever!

When I came home I plopped in the chair and groaned to get some atten-tion. Just then mom came in and said, "How was your day?"
I replied, "Slow."
"Want to tell me about it," she asked.
So I started by telling her about the three tests we had in a row. One in math, one in science, and one in history. Then we had to go to art, and you know how I hate art.
"So now I see," Mom said. Your day went slow because you had to do things you don't like.
"Yes, but no, because I also went to gym and recess and I love those."
"It sounds like you just had a bad day. Let me ask you, "did you get any sleep last night or eat a good brakefast this morning before you left?"
"No," I said. " Dad and I were watching 24 and I was late to the bus. So I guess your right. It started out bad and ended up worse!"
Just then I looked at the clock and noticed that it was 6:00. "OH NO! I'm late for my football game!"
Everyrthing piled up to one thing for sure. This was definitely the worse day of my life. And I learned something else. Talking about your bad day makes the time fly!

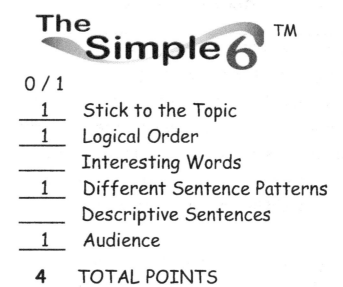

The Simple 6 ™

0 / 1

___1___ Stick to the Topic
___1___ Logical Order
_____ Interesting Words
___1___ Different Sentence Patterns
_____ Descriptive Sentences
___1___ Audience

4   TOTAL POINTS

Assessment Commentary:
This Score 4 sample gets points for Stick to the Topic, Logical Order, Sentence Patterns, and connecting with the Audience. There were not enough Interesting Words to get credit, and for a passing paper Descriptive Sentences did not have enough details in well-developed paragraphs.

As soon as I got home, I practically dragged myself to my big, leather, comfortable chair in the living room. I let out a big sigh, "Ahhhh," I said. Just as I grabbed the silver remote to turn on the plazma screen T.V., my mother skipped happily into the room. She is always happy, and sometimes it gets really aggravating, especially right now. "How was your day?" she asked me as if I seemed like I wanted to talk about it!

Then she just sat there and stared at me, with a gigantic smile from ear to ear on her pale face. So I told her the whole story, from the very beginning of the day. It went like this.

As soon as I got on the bus everyone was screaming and yelling and acting a lot worse than usual because we had a substitute busdriver. That commotion gave me a huge headache! Then instead of just sitting with my friend Avery, I had to sit with Jen too, who is not my friend at the moment. Plus, they never shut up!

After I got off the bus to go to breakfast I tripped and fell and scratched my arm pretty seriously. Then I kinda felt like crying, but didn't because I was too mad. Then when I finally got to breakfast they were having nasty stuff so I went to the before school room. I got in trouble by Mrs. Dean then, because I was supposabley running in the hallway.

Next the annoying bell rang and I couldn't get my locker opened. So I was a couple minutes late to math class. I got written up for that. After math, it was lunch-time, as usual. Today I got chocolate milk spilled all over me! How annoying! I had to go to the nurse's office and get a new pair of pants. You know how the nurse's office is. All of her pants are dorky, so I had to put on these pants that were way too big.

At the end of the day, to top it all off, my boyfriend breaks up with me. And that's just the highlights of why the day was so bad.

"Wow!" said my mom. That must have been offle. "It was," I said like it was so painful. So in conclusion, this is the worst day of my life. I'm so glad it's over.

The Simple 6 ™

0 / 1

__1__ Stick to the Topic

__1__ Logical Order

__1__ Interesting Words

_____ Different Sentence Patterns

__1__ Descriptive Sentences

__1__ Audience

5 TOTAL POINTS

Assessment Commentary:
This Score 5 sample needs some polishing on Sentence Patterns to get it to a Score 6.

The Longest Day of My Life

This story is about a kid who just returned from his job at the Orange County Orange Trees. . .

In a county called Orange County there was a boy named Tom Mason who just came back from the Orange County Orange Trees where he had been working for about a year. When Tom got home he threw off his mud crusted shoes and plopped on the chair and said, "This day was the longest day ever!"

His mom Tammy came around the corner and said, "Why do you say that?" I say that because today when I was working with Trent Crane he would never be quiet. I finally told him to shut up, and he slapped me in the face. I swung at him and broke his nose. He was crying so loud that everyone came running. The instructor came and walked us to his office and yelled at us like he was insane or something. It felt like it took two hours before those lips shut. "Any way, it wasn't really my fault. He just wouldn't shut up so I could do my work. And after that, the day went on and on. Everybody was looking at me like I caused it all."

"Wow, a lot did happen to you today," Tammy said in amazement.

I told my mom how exhausted I was after that. She said maybe I should lay down before dinner. I said it was probably a good idea, because "I was as cranky as a bear waking up in the winter".

That was the day that I thought was the longest, and I hope I don't wake up until tomorrow, when I head back to work at the Orange County Orange Trees.

The Simple 6 ™

0 / 1

__1__ Stick to the Topic

__1__ Logical Order

__1__ Interesting Words

__1__ Different Sentence Patterns

__1__ Descriptive Sentences

_____ Audience

5 TOTAL POINTS

Assessment Commentary:

This Score 5 sample Sticks to the Topic, has Logical Order, and has Interesting Words (such as instructor, insane, exhausted, and cranky). Different sentence patterns contribute to the overall fluency of the piece, and although there could be more details, Sentences are Descriptive. More improvement could be made on connecting with the Audience.

One winter day I trudged home from school, and it felt like the longest day of my life. I came in from the cool crisp air and plopped down in my chair. My mom zipped around the corner with my favorite food, grilled cheese sandwitch with tomato soup, mmmmm! Well, anyway she sat down next to me and asked how my day went, so I told her all the miserable details.

"It started this morning," I said, when I got on the bus the people were so incredibly loud. They just kept screaming their heads off!"

"Well, why didn't you tell them to quiet down a bit?" mom said.

"I did but they just kept on talking louder and louder and it gave me a really excrutiating headacke!

As soon as I got to school I headed straight for the nurses office and told her and she said "I can't give you anything so why don't you just go back to your classroom and lay your head down." So I did and it felt a little better. Then, doesn't it figure, we had to go to music. We had to sing all these dumb songs, and my headacke was back in about five minutes.

At lunch it was loud like it always is, but then it got worse. Joe and Tony, the two biggest trouble makers, got into a huge food fight. Everyone was screaming and the principal came to drag them away. Nobody settled down after that.

After that was recess but I stayed in to get caught up on work. At least it was quiet inside and things settled down a little bit. By math my headache was gone, but the day seemed so long. It was only 1:00 and I had three more classes to endure. In computer lab we completed our Powerpoint presentations and then we went to health. Health was really easy, because we just watched a movie about drugs. Truthfully, I think I took a little snooze during that one, but nobody noticed. History was easy but boring. We listened to a lesson out of the book and had time to work on our homework assignment.

On the way home, the bus seemed to be a little bit quieter, probably because Joe and Tony were in detention. Now I'm home, just hoping for a little relaxation so my headake will not come back.

"So, tell me Mom. How was your day?"

TM

The Simple 6

0 / 1

__1__ Stick to the Topic
__1__ Logical Order
__1__ Interesting Words
__1__ Different Sentence Patterns
__1__ Descriptive Sentences
__1__ Audience

6 TOTAL POINTS

Assessment Commentary:
This one has it all. It Sticks to the Topic, has Logical Order, and Interesting Words (trudged, incredibly, excrutiating, endured, and detention). Sentence Patterns contribute to the fluency of the reading, there are Descriptive Sentences, and the writer connects with the Audience.

It was finally over. I had managed to endure eight of the longest hours of my life! I had just gotten home and had settled in the big easy chair when mom came home from work. Of course, she wanted to have a conversation with me. So I told her about my day, which really had seemed like the longest day of my life.

When you come right down to it, there really wasn't anything out of the ordinary that happened. That's probably why it seemed so long.

My best friend John Kaiser felt the same way. We have the exact same class schedule, so we complained back and forth to each other all day. We have computer lab first thing, but the computers were down, so there was a wasted hour. Next we went to PE with a sub. That was total chaos. It wasn't boring, that's for sure, but when the class is out of control you don't get much done. Math went on and one and then it was time for lunch. They served macaroni and glue and that puts everyone in a bad mood.

Why did the day seem so long? BORING is the first thing that comes to my mind. Why can't any of our classes be fun? Why can't we ever do anything different? Why is the food so terrible? It doesn't seem like it should be too much to ask for school to be fun. We could do some games every now and then, watch a movie, have some science experiments. Whatever. Just not listening to teachers talk all day.

Mom said if it would make me feel better we could do something special, like go out to eat or to a movie. After all, I really didn't have much homework. So I said, "Great! Let's go to Steak and Shake" which we NEVER do during the week. After that the day didn't seem quite so bad.

The Simple 6 ™

0 / 1
__1__ Stick to the Topic
__1__ Logical Order
__1__ Interesting Words
__1__ Different Sentence Patterns
__1__ Descriptive Sentences
__1__ Audience

6   TOTAL POINTS

Assessment Commentary:
This Score 6 paper Sticks to the Topic, has Logical Order, and Interesting Words (endure, conversation, and chaos). Overall structure and details could be improved, but there is definitely evidence of Different Sentence Patterns, Descriptive Sentences, and a connection with the Audience.

The Gift

Read the information in the box. Then complete the writing activity.

Your best friend's birthday is next week, but you are broke! You want to show your friend how much he or she means to you, but you just can't afford anything really nice. What will you do instead of buying a present? What will your friend think? Why is the saying, "Sometimes the best gifts in life are free," appropriate for this story?

Write an essay about your dilemma. Be sure to tell what you will do instead of buying a present that costs money and how your friend reacted to the gift you gave. Be sure to include as many details as you can to make your article interesting.

Pre-Writing Activity

Plan your writing on other paper before you begin.
Be sure your story has a beginning, a middle, and an end.

Here are some questions to help you organize your story.
    What will you do instead of buying a present?
    What will your friend think?
    Why is the saying, "Sometimes the best gifts in life are free," appropriate for your
    story?

Add details to make your writing interesting.
Write on as many lines as possible. The length of your story should be more than one page.

Your writing will be scored on how clearly you write and how well you get your ideas across. Be sure to check over everything before you turn it in.

I will tell him that he is my friend and stay my friend.
My friend shoud still like me as a friend.

The Simple 6 ™

0 / 1
att 1 Stick to the Topic
_____ Logical Order
_____ Interesting Words
_____ Different Sentence Patterns
_____ Descriptive Sentences
_____ Audience

1   TOTAL POINTS

Assessment Commentary:
An attempt was made to write about the assigned topic, even though we do not see the word gift. One point only is given for attempting to Stick to the Topic.

I will bake a bach of cookies, now I have to ask my mom.

The Simple 6 ™

0 / 1

<u>att 1</u> Stick to the Topic

_____ Logical Order

_____ Interesting Words

_____ Different Sentence Patterns

_____ Descriptive Sentences

_____ Audience

1   TOTAL POINTS

Assessment Commentary:
An attempt was made to write about the assigned topic, even though we have to infer the connection. One point only is given for Sticking to the Topic.

I will just give him a gift that will play with him. He will like it he will have fun. He always calls me to play with him at his house. We play baseball or soccer.

The Simple 6 ™

0 / 1

att 1   Stick to the Topic

__1__   Logical Order

_____   Interesting Words

_____   Different Sentence Patterns

att 1   Descriptive Sentences

_____   Audience

2   TOTAL POINTS

Assessment Commentary:
In this Score 2 paper an attempt was made to write about the assigned topic and include some descriptive details. Details are not developed and an order is not apparent. Two points are given for attempting to Stick to the Topic and include Descriptive Sentences.

I want to buy my friend a gift. My friend's birthday is next week. I'm broke and I don't have a way to get any money. Then I had to make a present for her. I was scared she might not like it.

The Simple 6 ™

0 / 1
att 1 Stick to the Topic
_____ Logical Order
_____ Interesting Words
_____ Different Sentence Patterns
att 1 Descriptive Sentences
_____ Audience

2   TOTAL POINTS

Assessment Commentary:
An attempt was made to write about the assigned topic and include some descriptive details. With a conclusion, this paper had the potential to be a very low level Score 3. Points were given for Stick to the Topic and attempting to include Descriptive Sentences.

The Gift

My best friend's birthday is tomorrow, I can't believe I forgot about it. I have nothing to get her, because I have no money. This is going to be hard, but I think I will accomplish of throwing her a sleepover party at my place.

I will invite seven of her wonderful friends to it. I'm starting to decorate my house with left over stuff from my last year's birthday. I'm putting streamers and a sparkley banner that says "Happy Birthday". It will be a BIG surprise. She will love it.

All her friends will be there and scream out when she walks in "Happy Birthday Lindsey!" She will be so surprised because she thinks I didn't' remember when he birthday is, but I just remembered yesterday that's why I didn't have an important and ordinary gift. I think she will like my little party I'm throwing her.

Another thing I will invite Matt because she likes him and she will love me if I invite him and he comes. I will tell him after we scream very loudly "happy birthday", he will run up and give her a hug and wish her "Happy Birthday." She will like faint. She even told me that she didn't care if he got her anything, she just want him to come and wish her a happy Birthday.

He said he would come when I asked him and he said he would come and even get her a ring. She will be so happy that she will be static.

The Simple 6 ™

0 / 1
_1_ Stick to the Topic
_1_ Logical Order
____ Interesting Words
____ Different Sentence Patterns
att 1 Descriptive Sentences
____ Audience

3   TOTAL POINTS

Assessment Commentary:
In this Score 3 sample the writer sticks to the topic of the gift. Order is apparent but not as structured as it could be. Details are included but could be more developed and addressed in individual paragraphs. This is a typical Score 3 paper, receiving points for Stick to the Topic. Logical Order, and attempting Descriptive Sentences; but the paper is not really fluent or polished.

The Birthday Gift

My best friend Melissa is going to have a birthday party this week-end and I havn't got her a gift. I don't have any money neather so I will have to make her something but I don't know what to make her. I know what I will do I will ask her what she likes then I will see if what I can do. I know she likes make up and I just bought a new make up kit and I don't ware make up so I will give that to her and now I wont have to make her anything. The make up I am going to give her is lite because she don't like dark make up. I will put it in a red bag with red wraping paper. On friday I will go to her house and on saturday I will give her the preset. I hope she likes it.

The
Simple 6 ™

0 / 1
__1__   Stick to the Topic
__1__   Logical Order
_____   Interesting Words
_____   Different Sentence Patterns
att 1 Descriptive Sentences
_____   Audience

3   TOTAL POINTS

Assessment Commentary:
This is a very typical Score 3 paper, receiving points for Stick to the Topic, Logical Order, and including undeveloped Descriptive Sentences. Interesting Words are missing, sentence patterns do not contribute to the fluency of the reading, and a connection was never made with the audience.

It's Saturday morning so I wake up late. I open the window and it's a great day. Oh yea, it's the day of tom's party! I look at the clock its 1:00. Oh no the part starts at 1:00! So I have my mom run me over two tom's house but the party is all ready started.

When I walk into the party they look like they are opening gifts. Tom says "where's my gift Dave" I say "My family didn't have enough money I'm sorry I say. But he looks really mad.

Well its been 30 min. and we still haven't talked, so I walk over to him and say: the gift I want to give you is our friendship, but he still won't talk to me.

I guess I have tried my best so I go and sit outside on the steps. I start to cry because tom wonn't be my best friend. I think I might go home. I tell tom's mom I want to use the phone but as I get ready to dial I hear "wait". . .

I look behind me and I see tom he says "Hey Dave I'm really sorry about earler I was being a sore thumb. I agree with you friendship is the best gift any one could give. So for the rest of the party I have a great time with my best friend tom.

The Simple 6 ™

0 / 1

1	Stick to the Topic
1	Logical Order
___	Interesting Words
1	Different Sentence Patterns
1	Descriptive Sentences
___	Audience

4   TOTAL POINTS

Assessment Commentary:
This student gets points for Stick to the Topic. Logical Order, Sentence Patterns, and Descriptive Sentences. This is a lower level Score 4 because of the lack of structure within paragraphs, giving us fewer detailed descriptions than we would like to see at Grade 6.

Happy Birthday

One of my very best friends, Dani is having a birthday. Her birthday is next week and I'm flat out broke. I want her to know how much she means to me so I've decided to make a memory box of our friendship with old pictures and an old wooden box that used to be a cabinet.

I've tooken some old p8ictures out of a family album I put together four years ago and placed them inside the old cabinet, which I cleaned up and painted. I placed some bright pink lacing around the outside of the cabinet for decoration and some cloth in the inside of the cabinet. Now for the glass that is placed on the front of the cabinet. Finally I'm finished with my present.

I hope Dani likes my present and I hope she knows what a great, trustworthy, caring friend she is to me. Just like the phares "sometimes the best gifts in life are free." I really believe in that phares.

I think that phares is very true because friendship isn't something you buy with money, friendship is priceless. Friendship is a special bond between two people who trust and care for each other.

I just hope Dani knows she's a great friend and I hope she will accept my gift even if I didn't spend all my money. I just really want to show her all the good things and times we have shared together and I hope there are sooo many more to come!

The Simple 6 ™

0 / 1

__1__	Stick to the Topic
__1__	Logical Order
_____	Interesting Words
_____	Different Sentence Patterns
__1__	Descriptive Sentences
__1__	Audience

4   TOTAL POINTS

Assessment Commentary:
This Score 4 paper gets points for Stick to the Topic, Logical Order, Descriptive Sentences, and connecting with the Audience. While sentence patterns may seem to be differentiated, they do not contribute to the overall fluency of the piece.

The Gift

"Oh, no!" I said, when I discovered it was my friend's birthday, and I had no money. I asked my parents to lend me some money, but all they said was, "We don't have any to spare, sorry."

"But what will I do?" I asked.

"Don't worry, you have a week, you'll think of something."

So I sat up all that night thinking of what to get her. A bracelet, I thought? No, too worthless. A necklace? No, too useless. So I desided to make her a friendship book. She'll absolutely love it! I can't wait to get started!

The very next morning I got up at seven o'clock to get to work on it. I was so excited! I couldn't locate a photo album, but I remembered an old scrap book that I had gotten a few years ago. It was still empty, I knew that. I just had to find it. I reached up to the top shelf in my closet and all of a sudden I felt the smooth black box that it was in. I didn't get a good enough hold on it, though, and it came crashing down on me. Luckily, no one woke up. "Phew, that was a close one," I said out loud. My parents would kill me if I woke them up this early.

I spent all week working on the special gift for my friend, cutting, pasting, and gluing. I tried to think of all the things we had done in our lives. I had pictures of some, and I wrote about others. Finally it was time for the party. "I hope she feels the same way you do, that the best gifts can be free," I quietly said to my mom as she drove me to the party.

"I'm sure she will love your gift," my mother said encouragingly. "And I know she will appreciate all the time you spent on it. Sarah has been your best friend all your life."

"True. I just wish I would've had money," I said sadly.

It was time for Sarah to open her gifts. She grabbed my present and excitedly opened it. Tears ran down her cheeks. "What's wrong? Do you hate it?"

"No, I love it," she said happily. "It just reminds me of what a great friend you are," she said with a smie.

Since then all my friends are making homemade presents. Surprisingly my mom was right. She said, "Some of the best gifts can be free," and now I know why she said it. Sarah and I have been good friends our whole lives, and I think we'll be friends forever.

0 / 1

_1_	Stick to the Topic
_1_	Logical Order
____	Interesting Words
_1_	Different Sentence Patterns
_1_	Descriptive Sentences
_1_	Audience

5   TOTAL POINTS

Assessment Commentary:
This Score 5 paper, while not strong on structure and paragraph development, has all the components except Interesting Words. It wouldn't take much to make this a Score 5.

Best Gifts Being Free

One day when I was walking on the sidewalk I was humming to myself. When all of the sudden. . .I just remembered tomorrow was my best friends birthday. His name was Jon Hardy. He was going to turn eighteen. I had no money, so I had to figure out what I was going to get him. I soon discovered that being out of money is a big problem. I had to make sure his birthday present was tremendously awesome. So I decided that I was going to build him a car.

I knew somebody who owned a junkyard that could give me the parts I needed. I walked to the junkyard that was half a mile from where I was. When I arrived at the junkyard I told Jim, the guy in charge, about the situation. So he made a deal with me to trade some parts I already had and then drove me back to my house and I got started right away. I finished the car in thirty-six hours.

I built an outrageously, extreamly, through the roof, car. It has flames as the design, high drolex, nitrous, and can go over 250 miles per hour.

When I drove that car in the drive and he saw it he jumped through the roof. WOW! It's a really sweet, cool, awesome car. "Thank you!" Jon said. "Your welcome!" I said.

He asked me what best gifts being free ment to me. I asked him the same. We both agreed, "THERE THE BEST." That's how the party turned out. Also, I loved his smile.

The Simple 6 ™

0 / 1

1	Stick to the Topic
½	Logical Order
1	Interesting Words
1	Different Sentence Patterns
½	Descriptive Sentences
1	Audience

5   TOTAL POINTS

Assessment Commentary:
Deciding the points on this Score 5 paper was difficult. We know the writer Sticks to the Topic and establishes a connection with the Audience from the beginning. Interesting Words are recognized as tremendously, awesome, outrageously, extreamly, high drolex, and nitrous. Descriptive sentences take us through the first half of the story, but when it comes to the building of the car, we don't learn much. The story moves along in order, but the conclusion falls apart. Because of certain details being lacking or out of order, I give a half point to Logical Order and a half point to Descriptive Sentences.

The Gift of Friendship

One beautiful summer day I relized that my friend Ryan's birthday was presisly one week away. I was trying to decide what to get for him, but I didn't have any money. After thinking about it, I suggested that all his friends would meet at my house for an unexpected birthday party. Nobody had any money, so we each agreed to contribute something we had at home—like a frozen pizza, two liter pop, napkins, snacks, whatever we could find. And of course we asked our parents permission first.

May 11, the day of Ryan's birtyday, finally arrived. We had all agreed to meet at my house at 7 o'clock.   Six of us were all stuffed behind the couch in our family room and when Ryan came in we yelled, SURPRISE! Our friend was so astonished, he could hardly breathe! But as the party went on, he realized there weren't any presents. "Hey Brad," he whispered. "Where's the gifts?" We said, "We are the gifts!" Then I stood up and said, "The best gifts in the world are friends. Not toys and stuff. So here we all are on a Friday night, hanging out together, and everybody contributed something for the party even though we didn't really have any money."

"I guess your right," said Ryan. "I just never thought of it that way. So let's have some fun!" said the birthday boy. All the friends had a great time together for the rest of the party. We watched movies, played darts and ping pong, and devoured all the food everyone brought.   Today I still look back on that day and (usually) I think I did the right thing.

The Simple 6 ™

0 / 1
__1__ Stick to the Topic
__1__ Logical Order
__1__ Interesting Words
__1__ Different Sentence Patterns
__1__ Descriptive Sentences
__1__ Audience

6   TOTAL POINTS

Assessment Commentary:
 This Score 6 paper is well written but also pretty short for a Score 6. While it illustrates examples of all 6 components, improvement could be made in Descriptive Sentences by providing more details and "zooming in" on certain parts.

The Gift

My best friends birthday party is next week and I am broke! I knew I shouldn't have bought that skateboard ramp. I guess I could give it to him, but I worked too hard. I'm totally clueless! I have asked all my friends but they didn't know. What should I do? I guess I should think harder.

Two days before my friends birthday and I still have not gotten a present! I've asked my friends, my dad, my brother. But wait! I have not asked my mom. I should have thought of her first! When I found her in the basement doing laundry I said, "Mom, my friends party is Saturday and I still have no present! What should I get him that doesn't cost anything?"

"Maybe you should make him something. How about a card?" she said.

"Thank you, that's perfect!" I said. Then I ran to my room, sifted through the clutter to find some supplies, and started making him a colorful and beautiful card. People have told me I have talent as an artist, and I took a lot of time on this project. I did an ink drawing on the front of his dog, Rocket. My mom thought that the resemblance was remarkable! Actually, I thought it was pretty impressive myself. I just hoped that Dan thought so, instead of thinking I was just a cheapskate.

Finally it was Saturday, the day of my friends birthday. The day I would see if my friend would like his card. I think he will.

My mom dropped me off outside his gigantic house and I was even more nervous. It was finally time to open all the presents. I felt stupid, because everyone was giving him superb, wonderful gifts, and mine was everything but. He opened it up and that was the happiest look I've ever seen! Later he said my gift was the best, because after all, I'm his best friend. I told him how embarrassed I was that it didn't cost anything and then he said, "You have no idea how happy I am to get this gift, but I'm sad at the same time. Rocket has an inoperable tumor and will have to be put to sleep soon. I really appreciate having this drawing of him. And besides that, haven't you heard? The best gifts in life are free!"

The Simple 6 ™

0 / 1

1	Stick to the Topic
1	Logical Order
1	Interesting Words
1	Different Sentence Patterns
1	Descriptive Sentences
1	Audience

6   TOTAL POINTS

Assessment Commentary:
This is a strong Score 6 for a Grade 6 student.

Converting a Rubric Score to a Grade Book Score

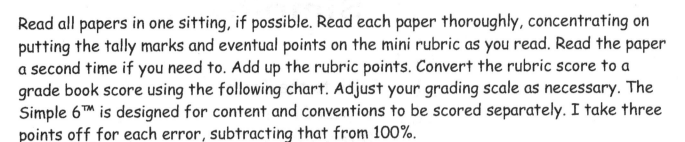

Read all papers in one sitting, if possible. Read each paper thoroughly, concentrating on putting the tally marks and eventual points on the mini rubric as you read. Read the paper a second time if you need to. Add up the rubric points. Convert the rubric score to a grade book score using the following chart. Adjust your grading scale as necessary. The Simple 6™ is designed for content and conventions to be scored separately. I take three points off for each error, subtracting that from 100%.

Grading Scale

Score 6: Content Rubric		
6	97-100	A+
5	90-96	A
4	80-89	B
3	70-79	C
2	60-69	D
1	below 59	F

A completed rubric might look like this.

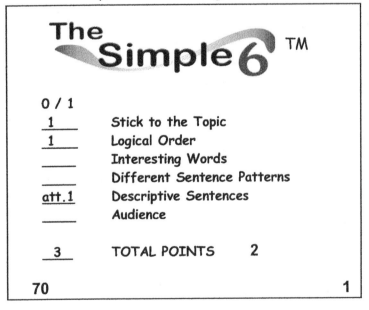

The mini rubrics on page 104 are designed to be cut into fourths. They should be attached to the front of each writing sample. They should also be readily available for student use.

Using Data to Drive Instruction

The class analysis chart should drive instruction after the initial nine-week implementation and every year after that. Its sole purpose is to give point spreads on each student so you can get the answers to the following questions:

What weaknesses do I see in the whole class that tell me I need to reteach a specific skill?

Which students need to be met with in flexible groups for skill reinforcement?

Which conventions issues need to be address to the whole class?

Which students need help with conventions either individually or in small groups?

Which students have the potential to get the Score 6?

What percentage of students is currently passing?

CLASS ANALYSIS CHART

PROMPT: *The Longest Day*   DATE *May, 2007*

NAMES	TOPIC	ORDER	WORDS	PATTERNS	DESCRIPT.	AUDIENCE	TOTAL
Abbot, C.	1	1	1				3
Bader, A.	1	conc.	1	1	1		4
Brady, S.	1	1					2
Brown, M.	1	conc.	1	1	1	1	5
Carey, T.	1	1		1	1		4
Chen, Y.	1	1			att. 1		3
Drake, M.	1	1		1	1		4
Gonzales,	att.	att.					2
Hall, D.	1	1	1	1	1		6

SYMBOLS: Left Side
R   Readability
SH Too Short
*   Score 6

SYMBOLS: Right Side
*   Punctuation Issues
""   Quotation Mark Issues
,   Comma Issues
¶   Indentation Issues
✓   Model Strategy

Comments:

Whole Group: *Focus on interesting words and audience/voice.*

Flexible Groups: *Meet with Bader, Brown, and Gonzales to work on conclusions.*
Meet with Abbot, Brady, Chen, and Gonzales for descriptive sent.
Focus on developing paragraphs.

CLASS ANALYSIS CHART

PROMPT: _____   DATE _____

NAMES	TOPIC	ORDER	WORDS	PATTERNS	DESCRIPT.	AUDIENCE	TOTAL

Comments / Reflection:

WRITING PROMPTS CLASS RECORD
GRADES 2-12

Year: _____   Teacher: _____

STUDENT NAMES	BASELINE:AUG. CONT (6) /CONV (4)	PROMPT 1:OCT. CONT (6)/CONV (4)	PROMPT 2: JAN. CONT (6) / CONV (4)	PROMPT 3:MAR. CONT (6) /CONV (4)	FINAL: MAY CONT (6) /CONV (4)
% PASSING APP./CONV.	/	/	/	/	/

Comparing Data for your Current Class

Teacher: _____

Date _____ Task _____

	Score 0 N	%	Score 1 N	%	Score 2 N	%	Score 3 N	%	Score 4 N	%	Score 5 N	%	Score 6 N	%
# of Students														
(6) Writing Application														
(4) Lang. Conventions														

% Passing · % Not Passing

Date _____ Task _____

	Score 0 N	%	Score 1 N	%	Score 2 N	%	Score 3 N	%	Score 4 N	%	Score 5 N	%	Score 6 N	%
# of Students														
(6) Writing Application														
(4) Lang. Conventions														

% Passing · % Not Passing

Date _____ Task _____

	Score 0 N	%	Score 1 N	%	Score 2 N	%	Score 3 N	%	Score 4 N	%	Score 6 N	%	Score 5 N	%
# of Students														
(6) Writing Application														
(4) Lang. Conventions														

% Passing · % Not Passing

Chapter 5 Revision
Teaching Students to be Responsible for their Own Revisions

Just Simple 6™ It! Beginning Checklist

Strategy #1 Small Group Revision
       Strategy #1 Samples

Just Simple 6™ It! Intermediate Checklist

Strategy #2 Triple Trade Off
       Strategy #2 Samples

Strategy #3 Partner Revision
       Strategy #3 Samples

Strategy #4 Self Evaluation
       Strategy #4 Samples

Just Simple 6™ It! Advanced Checklist

Chapter 5:   REVISION
Getting Students Involved in the Process

The purpose of revision is to improve the quality of the content (not to be confused with editing – which corrects mechanical errors). If students have an organized strategy for revision, they are less likely to be overwhelmed by the task. After all, they are being asked to improve a piece of writing that they thought was pretty good to begin with! Below is a checklist for students who are just beginning to learn how to revise their work.

JUST SIMPLE 6™ IT!
Beginning Checklist for Revision

STICK TO THE TOPIC
   Did I follow instructions, or did I choose my own topic?

LOGICAL ORDER
   Beginning: At the very least, did I tell what I was going to write about?

   End: Did I write more than one sentence or *THE END*?

   Middle: If there were questions in the prompt, did I answer them?

INTERESTING WORDS
   Did I go back and look for at least three words that could be improved?

SENTENCE PATTERNS
   Do my sentences all sound the same?

DESCRIPTIVE SENTENCES
   Did I use any words to describe?

© **Pieces of Learning**

Introductory Lesson: Modeling Beginning Revision Strategies

Use the Beginning Checklist for Revision to improve the samples on the next two pages.

The Best Pizza in the World   Grade 3 / Sample A: Score 3

This sample obviously was not organized around a Prompt Attack. Before you begin to look at that option with your class, read the paper, and see how much information you can learn from it. Then have your class score it.

Does it. . .

Stick to the Topic?	Yes. It's about pizza.
Have Logical Order?	No, the thoughts are not organized, and it is hard to follow.
Interesting Words?	Other than *condishoner*, no. Three are needed.
Sentence Patterns?	Yes, but they don't contribute to the overall fluency.
Descriptive Sentences?	Yes, a very small attempt, and they are hard to follow.
Audience?	Yes, we definitely feel his personality.

Where will you start? Take the information you know from the rough draft, and start placing the answers to the questions on a Prompt Attack. You will be rebuilding this story. Make sure students have a hard copy to follow while you model the Prompt Attack on an overhead and the rewrite on the board.

The Best Pizza in the World   Grade 3 / Sample B: Score 5

This student used the Prompt Attack strategy. While it is not a Score 6, it is much easier to follow and score than Sample 1. Always start with scoring.

Does it . . .

Stick to the Topic?	Yes. It's about pizza.
Have Logical Order?	Yes, it totally follows the prompt format.
Interesting Words?	Other than *ingreediants*, no. Three are needed.
Sentence Patterns?	Yes, even though there are a few structural problems.
Descriptive Sentences?	Yes, although there could be more.
Audience?	Yes, he attempts several times to connect with the audience.

Just Simple 6™ it! The writing is already structured. We know the major weakness is interesting words. Start by looking for three to replace. Where could there have been more details to make the vision clearer? Are all the reader's questions answered? This one will not take much, especially for Grade 3.

Sample A: The Best Pizza in the World

Your class is writing a book about favorite foods for kids, and pizza is your favorite food in the whole world! You would eat it every day if you could! What kind of pizza do you like best? Where does it come from? Why do you like it so much?

Write a story that describes the best pizza you have ever tasted.

Thursday is the best day of the week just waiting for pizza so I can gobble it all up. The best pizza in the world is from Papa's Pizza Place! I like it because it smells like hair condishoner. I took a bite. Oohh! That second bite really hit me right in the throat. Why did you get pepperoni pizza? Why not cheese? That's the best pizza in the world! The end.

0 / 1
____ Stick to the Topic
____ Logical Order
____ Interesting Words
____ Different Sentence Patterns
____ Descriptive Sentences
____ Audience

____ TOTAL POINTS

Sample B: The Best Pizza in the World

Your class is writing a book about favorite foods for kids, and pizza is your favorite food in the whole world! You would eat it every day if you could! What kind of pizza do you like best? Where does it come from? Why do you like it so much?

Write a story that describes the best pizza you have ever tasted.

Do you like pizza? Well, I love it! Every week we have the best pizza in the world! My favorite kind of pizza is sausij and mushroom with extra cheese. Everybody in my family gets the same kind and we get the biggest size of all. When the pizza man come to the door I can smell it already. My mouth is watering! The best pizza comes from Papa's Pizza Place. We always get are pizza from Papas. It is around the corner from my house, so they come about ten minits after we order it. My mama pays and my sister gets the paper towls. I like Papa's pizza the best because it taste so good! It has crunchy crust and just the rite amout of ingreediants. The cheese is always hot and gooey and the sausij is in little balls all over the top. That's the best pizza you will ever eat in your life.

0 / 1

____ Stick to the Topic
____ Logical Order
____ Interesting Words
____ Different Sentence Patterns
____ Descriptive Sentences
____ Audience

____ TOTAL POINTS

Follow up Lesson:
Model Beginning Revision Strategies AGAIN using different samples.

The Unusual Message   Grade 6 / Sample A: Score 3

This is a prime example of how hard it is to try to score a paper that contains dialogue that isn't in the proper form. It distracts the reader during scoring and confuses content. Overall, it feels like an outline to a story that seems to be missing many details.

Does it. . .

Stick to the Topic?	Yes. It's about an unusual message.
Have Logical Order?	Yes. There is an introduction, and a middle that is somewhat confusing, but I will deduct points elsewhere, and an abrupt conclusion.
Interesting Words?	No.
Sentence Patterns?	Yes, but they don't contribute to the overall fluency.
Descriptive Sentences?	This description would be considered an attempt for Grade 6.
Audience?	No.

Where will you start? Using the Prompt Attack, develop five paragraphs. Reread the rough draft, asking questions along the way that haven't been answered. That will help make the paper more descriptive. The middle is the sketchiest, so concentrate energy there. If choppy sentences are to remain, correct quotations marks must be inserted so the reader can tell that most of this is conversation. Definitely increase the level of vocabulary. Don't concentrate on audience/voice at this time.

The Unusual Message   Grade 6 / Sample B: Score 5

The connection with the audience is made immediately and maintains throughout the piece. Challenging vocabulary is apparent, so give those two points first. Depending on descriptive sentences, this may have Score 6 potential.

Does it. . .

Stick to the Topic?	Yes. It's about an unusual message.
Have Logical Order?	Yes. There is an introduction, a developed body, and a conclusion.
Interesting Words?	Yes. (persuasive, extraordinarily, conclusions, ominous. . .)
Sentence Patterns?	Yes, and they are very effective.
Descriptive Sentences?	Because this paper has the potential to be a Score 6, the scoring for descriptive sentences must be precise. There are unanswered questions and "holes" in the story. No point.
Audience?	Yes.

Make a list of questions that aren't clearly answered in this piece. Start by answering them, making sure the fluency of the story is not lost. Also, "the cat's pajamas" serves no real purpose as the conclusion. Consider embellishing or changing it.

Sample A: The Unusual Message

When you checked the phone messages after school today, there was one for you that said, "Meet me on the corner tonight at 9:00 p.m. Come alone. I have something for you." You did not recognize the voice, but it certainly sounded interesting. What will you do? Will you go? Will you tell someone?

Write a descriptive story that tells about your decision.

One day I came home from school I looked at our messages there was one for me. I could not believe what I had herd on the answer machine. It said meet me on the corner at 9:00 p.m. Well then it also said come alone. Be there. I have something for you.

Will I go or will I tell someone? So then after I listened to that awful message I was so scared I just kept wondering why someone would want to call me and leave such a hateful message for me. I have never been mean to no one in my life now that is very rude. So after a while I got on the phone and called my friend and told if there was ever a time that I would ever need her is now. She said what is wrong? Come over. You got to go with me to a corner. What corner? There are lots of corners and we will get caught. OK. We will pick one together. Now you make sure that you are over here by 8:30. Please, I'll be waiting on you.

She got there on time. We picked a corner and went there. She hid behind a trashcan and I went to see the guy. He held a big box in front of him and one hand behind him. What happens next?

0 / 1

____ Stick to the Topic
____ Logical Order
____ Interesting Words
____ Different Sentence Patterns
____ Descriptive Sentences
____ Audience

____ TOTAL POINTS

Sample B: The Unusual Message

When you checked the phone messages after school today, there was one for you that said, "Meet me on the corner tonight at 9:00 p.m. Come alone. I have something for you." You did not recognize the voice, but it certainly sounded interesting. What will you do? Will you go? Will you tell someone?

Write a descriptive story that tells about your decision.

"Click!" went the answering machine as I replayed the message in my head. "Meet me on the corner tonight at 9:00 p.m. Come alone. I have something for you." The voice was sinister but persuasive. The Corner, of course, was the most popular teen safe spot in town. It had an arcade, a video game system, a dance floor, and an extraordinarily tasty milkshake. But don't people usually say, "meet at" not "meet on"! Well, there's only one way to find out!

I decided to tell my mom I was going to The Corner to get a milkshake. Hey, I was part way telling the truth! I have to conclusions of who was on the answering machine. One, it was really a weirdo, or two, it was Buirkey playing an evil trick. I didn't find either threatening. Looking at the sky was no enjoyment that night. It was dark, cloudy, and ominous, not predicted by the whether man I might add. When I got there I asked Barney, the bartender for a milkshake, then started my search for this mysterious person. I found a curious looking character in the corner of The Corner. She indicated she wanted me to follow her up the stairs, and I hesitantly pursued.

It was raining now and I was soaked to the bone. There was a tent on the other side of the roof. Cautiously, I approached a vaguely familiar figure. Guess what? It was Carley, my best friend! She told me she had used a Darth Vader helmet with a voice changer to get an eerie voice. In the tent a bunch of my other friends were waiting for me. It was the cat's pajamas!

The Simple 6 ™

0 / 1

____ Stick to the Topic
____ Logical Order
____ Interesting Words
____ Different Sentence Patterns
____ Descriptive Sentences
____ Audience

____ TOTAL POINTS

Strategy #1: Small Group Revision / Same Writing Sample

Objective   Groups of 4-5 students will practice the strategies that were modeled during whole group instruction as the teacher observes, listens, and takes notes. Students will discuss and share their revisions with the rest of the class.

Materials   student writing sample on transparency

Instructional Sequence

The teacher will determine groups in advance. Consider having in the same group an "anchor" who is strong in language arts and a lower student who is struggling. All other group members should fit somewhere in between. Each group should have access to a projected or hard copy of the Revision Strategies.

Each group will determine the student roles.

    Student Roles: Discussion Leader
                    Group Writer (and later Reader)
                    Scoring Leader
                    Participants

Students will work together in small groups to improve the same writing sample. The goal will be to get it to a Score 6. The discussion leader will keep the group focused, making sure all students contribute. One student will write for the entire group.

After 10-15 minutes, a designated student will call on one group to share their revised story, usually by asking, "Which group thinks they have a Score 6?" The Group Writer will come forward with the revised transparency and read their group's revisions. All students in their seats will score the piece as it is read. That group's Scoring Leader will also come forward to discuss and validate the score at the end of the discussion.

Extra Questions the Scoring Leader might ask. . .

Stick to the Topic

    Did we answer all the questions?

Logical Order

    Which did you like better – our introduction or our conclusion?

Interesting Words

    What ARE the words?

Sentence Patterns

    How many different types do you see?

Descriptive Sentences

    Which strategies did we use?

Audience

    Where did we make connections with the reader?

Use the prompt on the next page to introduce Strategy #1 to your students.

Sample A: Crazy Creatures

Your class is writing a book called *Crazy Creatures*. Crazy creatures are animals that do amazing things that are crazy or silly. A crazy creature might be real or make believe. It might also be a real animal that does make-believe things.

Tell about an animal that you have seen, read about, or made up. What is the animal's name? What does it look like? What amazing things does it do? Why would other people think it is a crazy creature?

Once there was a crazy creature named Bob. Bob was a kangaroo with orange and brown fur and has the ability to jump 3,000 feet in the air. Why he does this, I don't now, but he can. How he does it, I do.

One day in the city of New York City where he lived, Bob jumped off the Twin Towers. he was a performer that did stunts. One day he jumped and went 3,000 fett in the air! From that day forward every time he took a step he went "up".

The solution was simple. He had to walk on stilts to keep from going in the air. Or did he. . .That's Bob the 3,000 feet jumping kangaroo!

0 / 1

____ Stick to the Topic

____ Logical Order

____ Interesting Words

____ Different Sentence Patterns

____ Descriptive Sentences

____ Audience

____ TOTAL POINTS

Sample B: Crazy Creatures

Your class is writing a book called *Crazy Creatures*. Crazy creatures are animals that do amazing things that are crazy or silly. A crazy creature might be real or make believe. It might also be a real animal that does make-believe things.

Tell about an animal that you have seen, read about, or made up. What is the animal's name? What does it look like? What amazing things does it do? Why would other people think it is a crazy creature?

Have you heard of a Snakopotumus? Well if you haven't you might need to know this. If you ever run into one make sure you have food for the creature because it is always hungry. And so you know what it looks like when you meet one, the front looks like a hippo and the back looks like a snake.

Though the Snakopotumus looks harmful it wouldn't hurt a fly. This creature is more afraid of you than you are of it. This creature can live underwater. And when this creature jumps it looks like a hippo balloon.

0 / 1

____ Stick to the Topic

____ Logical Order

____ Interesting Words

____ Different Sentence Patterns

____ Descriptive Sentences

____ Audience

____ TOTAL POINTS

Just Simple 6™ It!
Checklist for Intermediate Revision

Stick to the Topic
Did I stick to the topic and not run away with other ideas?
Did I answer or address all the questions in the prompt?

Logical Order
Beginning
Did I use a lead or hook to get my readers interested?
At the very least, did I mention the topic or title in my first paragraph?
Middle(s)
Is the body organized, probably by the questions in the prompt?
End
Is my conclusion more than one sentence?
Did I solve the problem, tell how things turned out, or review my main points?
Did I consider ending the piece with a reflection, opinion, or question?

Interesting Words/Challenging Vocabulary
Did I eliminate all overuse words such as went, said, big, little, and good?

Different Sentence Patterns
Does my essay or story sound like a list?
Did I vary my sentence patterns, using questions, exclamations, and series?

Descriptive Sentences
Did I name people, places, and tings with proper nouns?
Did I include adjectives – but not too many?
Did I give several detailed examples?

Audience
Did I write for a specific audience?
Did my personality shine through my writing?

Revision Strategy #2   Triple Trade Off

Objective: Students will work together in predetermined groups of three to improve   their individual writing.

Materials: student writing sample in writing folder
                   three sticky notes per student

Instructional Sequence:

After a whole group discussion on a particular revision strategy, students will return to their seats with their rough drafts in their writing folders.

<u>Step 1</u>: Each student will read his own piece, asking himself only a few questions.
     Did I stick to the topic? Did I answer all the questions in the prompt?
     Is my beginning inviting?
     Do I have a strong ending?
     Did I focus on today's revision strategy?
Write personal suggestions on one sticky note, and stick it on the back of the folder.

<u>Step 2</u>: Each student will pass his folder to the person to the right. Reading the piece, he will formulate a question or two that was not answered as he was reading. (examples: When did the story take place? What happened after. . .?) The student will write one or two questions on the sticky note and place it on the back of the folder.

<u>Step 3</u>: Pass the papers again to the next student. Read and ask one or two questions that will be written on the sticky note and placed on the back of the folder.

<u>Step 4</u>: The folders have now been returned to the original owner who has at least three ideas for revision without the teaching having been involved.

<u>Step 5</u>: Students work on their personal revisions, asking for assistance from their peers or the teacher who is circulating from group to group. Once students have revised (and edited) their pieces, they will recopy them in ink and turn in their writing folders.

This 60-minute activity is usually broken down as follows:

9:00 – 9:20   Teacher reviews a revision strategy based on yesterday's skimming of rough drafts. She checks for student understanding before returning student writing folders.

9:20 – 9:30   Students rotate papers, edit, and write comments on sticky notes.

9:30 – 9:45   Students make revisions, possibly interacting with group members.

9:45 – 10:00 Students copy final draft.

Student #1: How to Make a Bed

Your mom has just come into your bedroom and decided you need to clean it up. She tells you to start by making your bed. She is going into your twin brother's room next, and you know he has never even thought about making a bed!

Write a note to your brother that gives step-by-step instructions for your brother to follow so he will not get in trouble. How, exactly, do you make a bed? What should it look like when you're finished?

Dear Ray,

This is how you make a bed. first you set your covres and spred it on your bed. Then you straten the blanket out.

After that take the pillows and put them netlly on the bed.

Sinserly,

Seth

0 / 1
____ Stick to the Topic
____ Logical Order
____ Interesting Words
____ Different Sentence Patterns
____ Descriptive Sentences
____ Audience

____ TOTAL POINTS

Student #2: How to Make a Bed

Your mom has just come into your bedroom and decided you need to clean it up. She tells you to start by making your bed. She is going into your twin brother's room next, and you know he has never even thought about making a bed!

Write a note to your brother that gives step-by-step instructions for your brother to follow so he will not get in trouble. How, exactly, do you make a bed? What should it look like when you're finished?

Dear Austin,

Our Mom told us to clean our rooms today and I know thet you never maid your bed before so this is how to make your bed. First you pull up all three blankets. Next you put the one pillow on the bed face up. Last you get all the rinkles out. That's how to make a bed.

Your brother,
Tony

0 / 1
____ Stick to the Topic
____ Logical Order
____ Interesting Words
____ Different Sentence Patterns
____ Descriptive Sentences
____ Audience

____ TOTAL POINTS

Student #3: How to Make a Bed

Your mom has just come into your bedroom and decided you need to clean it up. She tells you to start by making your bed. She is going into your twin brother's room next, and you know he has never even thought about making a bed!

Write a note to your brother that gives step-by-step instructions for your brother to follow so he will not get in trouble. How, exactly, do you make a bed? What should it look like when you're finished?

Dear Bradley,

    I have some tips to give you on how to make a bed so you won't get in trouble! First you have to pull the sheets all the way back so you can make sure there aren't any wrinkles when you're done. That's my little secret. Shhhh! One by one you take the covers and smooth them out. If you have any stuffed animals you could lay them out nicely. Be carful! You know how much mom can be picky!

                Love, Paige

The Simple 6 ™

0 / 1
____ Stick to the Topic
____ Logical Order
____ Interesting Words
____ Different Sentence Patterns
____ Descriptive Sentences
____ Audience

____ TOTAL POINTS

Revision Strategy #3   Partner Revision

Objective   Students will work together in pairs to improve their individual writing.

Material   student writing sample in writing folder
Simple 6™ mini rubric

Instructional Sequence

After a whole group discussion on a particular revision strategy, students will return to their seats with their rough drafts in their writing folders.

Step 1: Each student will trade papers with his partner, and score the partner's paper using the Simple 6™ mini rubric. Return the scored paper to the owner. Discuss weaknesses that need to be improved.

Step 2: The student will then read his own paper, making adjustments and revisions along the way.

Step 3: The two students will alternate between writing and discussing improvements. The teacher circulates throughout the room during this exchange, focusing on asking questions to enhance writing – rather than making suggestions about what needs to be improved. During this time, students may also call the teacher over for assistance. When the owner is satisfied that the writing is his personal best, he will develop a final copy to turn in.

NOTE: Make sure you have taken the time to talk about the quality of a final draft paper.
What kind of paper will be used? (Will spiral "tear offs" be accepted?)
Should papers be written in cursive?
If copies are required to be in ink, do students have erasable pens?
Have you shown students where the (full) name and date go?
Should the title be centered?
Do you expect students to skip a line before they indent and begin?
Have you talked to students about how to create a right hand margin?
Did you remind students to write on the front side of the paper only?
   (very important for display purposes. . .)

Students will always perform to higher expectations, but you must tell them what your expectations are and slowly walk them through it the first time.

Partner 1: The Gift

Your best friend's birthday is next week, but you are broke! You want to show your friend how much he or she means to you, but you just can't afford anything really nice.

What will you do instead of buying a present? What will your friend think? Why is the saying "sometimes the best gifts in life are free" an appropriate saying? Write an essay about your dilemma.

My friend Joe will be having his birthday in two weeks but I can't get him anything good because I don't have any money. I think that the saying, "sometimes the best gifts in life are free" would come in handy at this time. I would make Joe a cookbook of my own recipes because Joe loves to cook.

I think that Joe would love this because, I'm sory to say, but Joe can't cook. If I give Joe a cookbook he would be delighted!

The Simple 6 ™

0 / 1
____ Stick to the Topic
____ Logical Order
____ Interesting Words
____ Different Sentence Patterns
____ Descriptive Sentences
____ Audience

____ TOTAL POINTS

Partner 2: The Gift

Your best friend's birthday is next week, but you are broke! You want to show your friend how much he or she means to you, but you just can't afford anything really nice.

What will you do instead of buying a present? What will your friend think? Why is the saying "sometimes the best gifts in life are free" an appropriate saying? Write an essay about your dilemma.

Discovering that I was broke, I knew I had to think of some way to honor my friend on her birthday. I know "the best things in life are free" but what should I give her? Family, friendship and love are not bought by money—how should I show that our friendship is important to me? I realize so many times that fake friendship is bought and a true friend can only be won by one's heart.

After much thinking I decided that friendship is created by kindness, respect, and best of all fun! So why not show my kindness and respect toward my friend even more? Enjoying each other's company, having fun, and making memories that will last a lifetime.

A true friend will not care whether I do not have enough money to buy a present. I mean as they say—it's the thought that counts!

0 / 1

____ Stick to the Topic
____ Logical Order
____ Interesting Words
____ Different Sentence Patterns
____ Descriptive Sentences
____ Audience

____ TOTAL POINTS

Revision Strategy #4 Self Evaluation

Objective: Students will work alone to improve their writing by attacking the prompt and Simple 6™ ing their work.

Materials: student writing sample in writing folder
Simple 6™ mini rubric

Instructional Sequence:

After a whole group discussion on a particular revision strategy, students will return to their seats with their rough drafts in their writing folders.

Each student will take time to read his paper thoroughly, and score it with The Simple 6™ mini rubric. He will focus on the following questions as he scores:

- Did I stick to the topic? If there was a prompt, did I answer all the questions?

- Does my introduction have a hook? Did I set the stage for my writing?

- Did I present my ideas in an order that is easy to follow?

- Is my conclusion more than one sentence?

- Did I improve at least three vocabulary words?

- Does my story sound like a list? What kinds of sentence patterns did I use?

- Did I use several strategies for descriptive writing?

- precise verbs

- proper nouns

- adjectives

- appeal to the reader's senses

- Did my personality come through the writing? Did I connect with the reader?

Student Rough Draft: My Favorite Food

Your class is making a book of their favorite recipes. Describe your favorite food. Why do you like it so much? Do you know how to make it? If not, who makes it for you?

Write a story that describes your favorite food.

I've tried tons of food but this is one that really stands out. Spicy orange chicken with a side of egg-drop soup! It's quite a unique taste a child is blessed with!

I enjoy spicy orange chicken because of its spicy flavor blasts. The enjoyable egg-drop soup is in the interdiction, cause it's mild, yet a spectacular taste of not just every-day soup.

There is something in orange chicken that is so hidden that I don't even know it, but if I did know the bazare taste, the secret would be out like that! (snap!)

Thank you for asking about my favorite food. It may be silly, but there's one thing I want to say. . .I love orange chicken and egg-drop soup!

The Simple 6 ™

0 / 1
____ Stick to the Topic
____ Logical Order
____ Interesting Words
____ Different Sentence Patterns
____ Descriptive Sentences
____ Audience

____ TOTAL POINTS

Student Final Draft: My Favorite Food

Your class is making a book of their favorite recipes. Describe your favorite food. Why do you like it so much? Do you know how to make it? If not, who makes it for you?

Write a story that describes your favorite food.

In my life I've tried tons of food (some delightful and some hateful) but this is one that really stands out. Spicy orange chicken with a side of egg-drop soup! I know it's quite a unique taste for a child to be blessed with, but that doesn't mean it can't be the most out-rageously scruptceos food in the universe!

I enjoy spicy orange chicken because of its spicy flavor blasts. It feals like an eruption of spicy goodness that floods your mouth for one minute each! If you don't have a craving for spine-tingling goodness with fireworks of over possably 500 spices then make sure you pack a gallon of water!

The enjoyable egg-drop soup is in the interdiction, cause it's mild, yet a spectacular taste of not just every-day soup. It is really a Chinese cultured secret untold. There is also an ingritient in orange chicken that is so hidden that I don't even know it, but if I did know the bazare taste, the secret would be out like that! (snap!)

Thank you for asking about my favorite food. It may be silly, emousenal, or enpresive, but there's one thing I want to determan. . .I love that outrageously delicious orange chicken and egg-drop soup!

The Simple 6 ™

0 / 1
____ Stick to the Topic
____ Logical Order
____ Interesting Words
____ Different Sentence Patterns
____ Descriptive Sentences
____ Audience

____ TOTAL POINTS

Just Simple 6™ It!   Checklist for Advanced Revision

Stick to the Topic

Did I stick to the topic and not run away with other ideas?

Did I answer or address all the questions in the prompt?

If there were no questions, did I design my own questions?

Logical Order

Beginning

Did I use a lead or hook to get my readers interested?

Did I develop a setting OR give an overview of what I was going to write about?

At the very least, did I mention the topic or title in my first paragraph?

Middle(s)

Is the body organized, probably by the questions in the prompt?

Does each paragraph address a new question?

End

Is my conclusion more than one sentence?

Did I lead into the end of the story or essay?

Did I solve the problem, tell how things turned out, or review my main points?

Did I consider ending the piece with a reflection, opinion, or question?

Interesting Words/Challenging Vocabulary

Did I eliminate all overused words such as *went, said, big, little,* and *good*?

Did I go back and look for three more opportunities to use challenging vocabulary?

Are my new words used correctly?

Different Sentence Patterns

Does my essay or story sound like a list?

Did I vary my sentence patterns, using questions, exclamations, and series?

Did I write compound and/or complex sentences?

How many sentences started with prepositional, adverbial, or participial phrases?

Do my sentences have smooth transitions?

Descriptive Sentences

Did I create a vision for the reader that matches what I see in my head?

Did I use precise verbs?

Did I name people, places, and things with proper nouns?

Did I include adjectives—but not too many?

Did I appeal to the reader's senses?

Did I give several detailed examples?

Audience

Did I write for a specific audience?

Did my tone match the prompt?

Did my personality shine through my writing?

Chapter 6   Administrative Leadership

Your School Improvement Plan

The School Administrator's Role
>   Reflection
>   Suggestions
>   Serious Questions

The Teacher's Role
>   Reflection and Self Evaluation

The Parents' and Community's Role

Celebrating Your Success

The Simple 6 ™

Chapter 6 Administrative Leadership

Your School Improvement Plan

School improvement plans are designed to encourage schools to take a close look at what they are doing, and evaluate whether or not the strategies currently being used are working. Schools typically identify three goals on which to work. How might these goals be determined? Test scores, student grades, teacher feedback, and staff, student, and parent surveys. Once writing improvement has been identified as one of your school's goals, you need to decide what you are going to do to improve and how you will track progress.

GOAL   to improve student writing achievement across the curriculum.

STRATEGY to implement The Simple 6™ writing program, using it as a guide for instruction and a means of local assessment.

Before you decide what you need to do to improve, you should ask yourself what you are currently doing and why it isn't working. Finally, in terms of standardized assessment, where do you stand? Is your current situation critical? Are some classes or grade levels doing better than others? If so, why?

The School Administrator's Role
  ➢ familiarize yourself with the program
  ➢ observe instruction
  ➢ offer additional assistance for those who need it
  ➢ collect and analyze data regularly
  ➢ motivate your staff and students
  ➢ find time for teachers to collaborate
  ➢ inform others of progress being made
  ➢ plan ahead for additional staff development training

The Teachers' Role
  ➢ collect baseline writing data
  ➢ implement the total nine-week program during one grading period
  ➢ self evaluate at the end of each grading period
  ➢ score student work using the mini rubric
  ➢ track data
  ➢ stay committed and enthusiastic
  ➢ empower students
  ➢ write across the curriculum

The Parent and Community's Role
  ➢ know the components of The Simple 6™
  ➢ be available to read your child's work
  ➢ provide assistance at school
  ➢ help spread the word

© **Pieces of Learning**

The School Administrator's Role
Reflection Page

Begin at the beginning.
How did you determine writing improvement to be a school-wide goal?

_____

_____

_____

_____

What does your baseline data tell you? When was it collected?

_____

_____

_____

_____

In terms of The Simple 6™ intervention, what is your immediate goal?

_____

_____

_____

_____

How can your instructional leadership guide the process of improving student writing achievement? The following list of suggestions may help get you started.

_____

_____

_____

Suggestions for School Administrators or Curriculum Leaders

1. **Familiarize yourself with the program.**
   Did you attend the staff development training with your staff?
   If not, what can you do to become more familiar with the instructional aspect of the program?

   _____

   _____

   _____

   _____

2. **Observe instruction.**
   Have teachers turned in their weekly lesson plans so you know when writing is being taught? _____

   When was the last time you dropped in on a lesson? _____

   How can you help teachers organize instruction?

   _____

   _____

   _____

3. **Offer additional assistance to those who need it.**
   Determine where instructional weaknesses are. Who needs assistance?

   _____

   _____

   - Suggest that the teacher "follow the plans in the book."
   - Check management skills. Is the schedule consistent? Do students have folders?
   Is feedback given immediately? Are students being empowered?
   - Make time for teachers to observe one another.
   - Open up discussion of trouble spots at grade level meetings so others can offer suggestions.

4. **Collect and analyze data.**

    Ask for quarterly feedback, either with the Self-evaluation Chart or the Comparing Data for your Current Class Chart (or both).

    _____

    _____

    _____

    How will teachers be held accountable? _____

    Check the quarterly progress that is noted on the Comparing Data Chart.

    _____

    _____

    _____

    _____

    _____

5. **Motivate staff and students.**

    What can you do to motivate the staff and students?

    _____

    _____

    _____

6. **Inform others of progress being made.**

    When visitors walk into your building, how do they know you value writing? _____

    Is time regularly set aside to report quarterly progress at staff meetings or administrative team meetings with central office administrators? It only takes a minute, but it lets everyone know you are staying on top of the situation.

7. **Find time for teachers to collaborate with one another.**

    What tasks might you ask teachers to do during an independent staff development session that is designed for collaboration? Here are some ideas.

Peer Collaboration Time for Teachers

✓ Create student folders.

✓ Write grade-level appropriate prompts.

✓ Score and discuss student writing samples.

✓ Think of ways to integrate writing with content areas.

✓ Plan vertical articulation.

✓ Discuss necessary documents for accreditation.

✓ Plan/write school-wide quarterly prompts.

✓ Collect/graph current data.

✓ K-1 teachers, plan picture book connections.

✓ K-1 teachers, plan descriptive drawing lessons.

✓ Brainstorm ideas for celebration/motivation.

8. **Plan ahead for future staff development training.**

    What short-term plans are already in place?_____
    _____
    How should you best organize for summer school and standardized testing? _____
    _____
    Where should you go from here so you don't lose momentum?
    _____

© **Pieces of Learning**

Some serious questions for teachers and administrators . . .

Instruction

- Have you honestly implemented the program (week by week, over 9 consecutive weeks)?
- Do you have a regular, consistent (writing) schedule that works for you?
- Do you understand each component?
- Can your students recite the 6 components and tell what each one means?
- Are students leading the review and working in peer groups to discuss revision?
- Are mini lessons being taught at the beginning of each writing session?
- Are writing topics related to current instruction?
- Are old pieces periodically revisited, discussed, and revised?

Scoring

- Do you understand it?
- Are you using the mini rubrics?
- Are students actively engaged in scoring?
- Are students getting weekly feedback about their writing?
- Are (quarterly) prompts being done, scored, and reviewed?
- Are (report card) grades given for writing?

Data

- Are you using the Class Analysis Chart to chart Prompt scores?
- Are you using analysis information to impact instruction?
- Have you identified large group weaknesses?
- Have you used your class data to create flexible groups for teacher intervention?
- Are you tracking local and standardized scores on your class? For each student?
- Have you identified your Score 1 and 2, your Score 3, and your passing students?

Attitude, Commitment, and Accountability

- Do you teach writing with enthusiasm and encouragement?
- Have you empowered students in the process?
- What motivational strategies are you using to keep students' interest?
- Are you keeping careful records?
- Are your records being checked, and is progress being reported?
- Have any of your writing lessons been observed?
- Is writing from all students displayed in your classroom – and changed frequently?
- Are outstanding and improved writers being recognized?
- Are grade level teachers rallying together for success?
- Are enthusiastic, successful writing teachers being recognized?

The Teachers' Role

1. Before you begin the program, or before you begin each school year, collect base line writing data. Use a prompt or a general writing topic, but all students should be writing about the same thing. Make copies of the student samples and file them in your Baseline Writing Folder.

   Date accomplished: _____

2. Implement the total nine-week program during one grading period. Unless you are a Grade 2 teacher, you will only do this one time – the first year the program is started. After that, you will simply review components at the beginning of the school year.

   Date review completed: _____

3. Schedule Prompt or focused writing on Thursday or Friday if possible and keep this same time throughout the year. Write to a Prompt or focus on particular skill weaknesses every other week. On the off weeks continue the same format, write across the curriculum, or use the time for a Writer's Workshop.

   Is your weekly schedule in place? _____

4. Score student papers immediately and in one sitting.
   Use the mini rubrics that will be attached to the writing sample.
   Transfer rubric scores to % scores for your grade book. (4 per grading period)

   Do you feel comfortable with the scoring? _____

5. Transfer rubric scores to the Class Analysis Chart.
   Use the Class Analysis Chart to guide whole group instruction and to create flexible groups for skill remediation.

   Do you understand how to use this data to drive instruction? _____

6. Track quarterly progress on the Comparing Data for your Current Class Chart. If your entire student body is writing to one prompt each quarter, that prompt should be used for the quarterly score. A copy of the Comparing Data Chart should be made and forwarded to the school data team or your administrator.

   Do you have a separate folder for tracking data? _____
   Do you know where you currently stand? _____

7. Empower students.
   Are students leading reviews, discussions, and revision sessions?

© **Pieces of Learning**

Teacher Reflection and Self-evaluation
How My Class is Doing Using The Simple 6™

Stick to the Topic: Great ___   OK ___   Didn't attempt ___

_____

_____

Logical Order: Great ___   OK ___   Didn't attempt ___

_____

_____

Interesting Words: Great ___   OK ___   Didn't attempt ___

_____

_____

Sentence Patterns: Great ___   OK ___   Didn't attempt ___

_____

_____

Descriptive Sentences: Great ___   OK ___   Didn't attempt ___

_____

_____

Audience: Great ___   OK ___   Didn't attempt ___

_____

_____

I integrated reading   Great ___   OK ___   Didn't attempt ___
with writing topics.

_____

_____

I integrated drawing   Great ___   OK ___   Didn't attempt ___
lessons to enhance
descriptive writing.

_____

_____

I saw the most improvement in _____.
We still need to focus on _____.

Teacher Name: _____ Grade: ___ Date: _____

The Parents' and Community's Role

1. Be available to provide assistance.

Volunteer to help out in classrooms. Come during the time that instruction will be given so you can learn more about The Simple 6™.

Try to make yourself available to read your child's work or to come in during the day to read other students' work.

If you feel capable, offer to help work with small revision groups.

Become proficient at scoring, so you can help teachers with multiple, departmentalized classes get immediate feedback to their students.

Help to spread the word about how your child's school is focusing on writing.

Help with making bound books so students have at least one published work each year.

2. Help to celebrate success.

Learn about writing contests that your child's school might enter.

Consider sponsoring the contest.

Offer to make simple writing awards, such as certificates or bookmarks.

Donate healthful snacks for the class that makes the most progress for the quarter.

3. Spread the word throughout the community.

Find venues throughout the community that are willing to display student writing.

Call the newspaper or TV station when something exciting happens that is related to writing.

Take pictures of writing projects or students working together on writing.

Create a writing bulletin board in the public library or youth center in your town.

Sponsor contests to encourage students to write more and to write better.

Celebrating Your Success and Spreading the Word

Once you and your students have experienced success, (and you will be successful), there are many things you can do to challenge others in your school or district.

Additional Training in The Simple 6™ Method

Like students, teachers learn more effectively with guidance and interactive experiences. Three levels of training are available in The Simple 6™ method of scoring writing assessments.

Peer Coaching Between Classes

Peer coaching is successful with students of the same age. It is a unique opportunity for teachers of the same grade level to create flexible groups with more than one class. Peer coaching is also effective when older students teach the younger students. Groups as well as partners can change every week.

In-house Staff Development Sessions

Once one or several of your school's teachers become proficient in The Simple 6™ method, use staff development days to peer coach one another! Spend 10 minutes at each staff meeting trying one of the strategies or discussing those that have really encouraged students to write.

Monthly Grade Level Meeting Discussions

If your district has monthly grade level or department meetings, take that opportunity to review and discuss the components of The Simple Six. Devise a grade level plan that is vertically articulated throughout the school district. Share successes. Develop anchor papers for each grade level.

Analysis and Display of Data

Collecting data is meaningless if there is never an opportunity to study and analyze it. School administrators need to take a leadership role in providing guidance and opportunities for teachers to analyze, discuss, and display their data.

School Improvement Team Awareness

If your school has a School Improvement Team, those teachers on the Writing Committee would be responsible for collecting and comparing quarterly data, suggesting school-wide writing prompts, and offering praise and suggestions.

Quarterly Teacher-Principal Conferences

This is an opportunity for each teacher in the building to meet with the principal to discuss areas of concern or to share successes of the writing program. This meeting also gives teachers the extra push that is needed to compile the data each quarter and have it ready for presentation.

Classroom Writing Centers

Classrooms should have many writing tools available to students. Notebooks, journals, chart paper, drawing paper, pictures, thesauruses, dictionaries, trade books, pencils, pens, markers, and sticky notes, should be in a Student Writing Center and readily available for use.

School-wide Writing Displays

All classes should be encouraged to display their writing: in their classrooms, outside their classrooms, in the cafeteria, in the principal's office, or anywhere else deemed appropriate. Schools may also choose to have a monthly or quarterly theme for which all students write to similar prompts or about similar subjects.

Class/School Recognition Programs and Parties

Students should be recognized as soon as they have reached the "passing zone," or Score 4. When an entire class is scoring 4 and above, it is time for a celebration. Check with your principal for grant money that may be available for rewards, or contact your local fast food restaurant. Many will be glad to help you celebrate.

"Real" Publication

Every now and then writers surface in the classroom who have pieces that should be considered for "real" publication. Many periodicals and journals publish student work. You may also find that your public library would be happy to display exemplary writing during National Education Week or some other appropriate time. Students who become proficient at persuasive writing might want to write a letter to the editor of the local newspaper. They are always happy to include well-written student letters.

Parental Involvement

Using volunteers from the community increases 1:1 assistance, especially with young writers. Parents and grandparents are happy to listen to students read their stories. They can also be taught to ask strategic questions that encourage students to think and expand their writing experiences.

District Recognition

Find a reason to celebrate writing across your school district. Monthly school board meetings are a wonderful opportunity to showcase the primary, intermediate, and secondary "Author of the Month." A simple certificate is a great motivator and an indicator that writing is valued in the school district.

Young Authors' Conference

Many school districts or Reading Associations sponsor Young Authors' Conferences. Students of all ages attend the conference, bringing a piece of their best writing to share. They usually attend three sessions: one by a children's author, another by an illustrator, and a final session in which they are asked to share their work with their peers.

Writers' Workshops

Writers Workshops in the classroom are becoming increasingly popular with the emphasis on balanced literacy. Students are given regular opportunities to write. They are encouraged to make choices, take risks, and explore various aspects of writing. Work in progress is kept in organizers so that students have easy access to pieces that they may want to take to the publishing stage.

Summer School Creative Writing Classes

Summer school is not just for remediation. Offering a creative writing class as a summer school option gives budding authors a chance to continue to write during the summer. It also allows them to meet new friends who are also interested in writing. A great culminating activity would be to have every student submit something to a children's literary magazine.

Writing Buddies in Another School

What could be more fun than starting the school year with a pen pal in another school? As the year progresses, students can be encouraged to share other pieces of their best writing, discuss novels or poetry, or offer writing topic ideas to one another. Meeting quarterly would give students a chance to meet, share their work, and have interactive writing projects or discussions.

Celebrating your Success and Spreading the Word from **Writing: The Simple 6™** *p. 184-186.*

Conclusion

The Simple 6™ has helped students all across the United States to focus on the elements of exemplary writing. The beauty is in the design – a simple analytic rubric that students as young as first or second grade can understand and explain to others. Teachers who have implemented the program see students who are confident and focused. Because they have a clear understanding of what is expected, writing skills show improvement within the first few weeks.

The Simple 6™, though, is like anything else that we teach. If we don't continue to give students opportunities to write, they won't improve their skills. If we don't continue to model strategies, they will forget what is expected at the highest level. If we don't continue to encourage them, they will lose interest. If we don't continue to give them feedback, they won't be able to take advantage of our expertise. The alternative is – we must continue to analyze the data, present lessons with enthusiasm, tie writing lessons to students' interests, stay on a consistent schedule throughout the entire year, and always ask, "Did you Simple 6™ it?"

Writing is a lifelong skill, and each teacher's contribution to a student's improvement and confidence is critical. The significance of The Simple 6™ to teachers is:

It doesn't matter if you're a six-year-old writing your first story, an eighteen-year-old taking the SAT, or an adult writing a note to his child's teacher . . .

If you **STICK TO THE TOPIC** in your writing, the reader will focus on the main idea.

If you have structured your writing with **LOGICAL ORDER**, the reader will be able to follow and understand your message.

If you include **INTERESTING WORDS** (challenging vocabulary), you will sound as intelligent as you really are.

If you have chosen **DIFFERENT SENTENCE PATTERNS**, your writing will not sound like a list.

If you have written **DESCRIPTIVE SENTENCES**, the reader will be able to visualize what you are trying to say.

If you have connected with the **AUDIENCE**, then what you have written has made an impact.

Just Simple 6 ™ It!

Resources

Clayton Heather. (2003) Great genre writing lessons. NY: Scholastic Professional Books.

Codell, Esme Raji. (2003) How to get your child to love reading. Chapel Hill: Algonquin Books.

Davidson, Kay. (2005) Using bloom's taxonomy to ask over 100 higher-level questions. Marion, IL: Pieces of Learning.

Davidson, Kay. (2003) Writing: the simple 6™. Marion, IL: Pieces of Learning.

Davidson, Kay and Decker, Tressa. (2006) Blooms and beyond: higher level questions and activities for the creative classroom. Marion, IL: Pieces of Learning.

Fountas, Irene C. and Pinnell, Gay Su. (2001) Guiding readers and writers grades 3-6: teaching comprehension, genre, and content literacy. Portsmouth, NH: Heinemann.

Freeman, Judy. (2006) Books kids will sit still for 3: a read aloud guide. Westport, CT: Libraries Unlimited.

Jacobs, James S. and Tunnel, Michael O. (2004) Children's literature,briefly: third edition. Upper Saddle River, NJ: Pearson Prentice Hall.

Kohl, MaryAnn F. (2003) Storybook Art. Bellingham, WA: Bright Ring Publishing, Inc.

Lane, Barry. (1999) Reviser's Toolbox. Shoreham, VT: Discover Writing Press.

Martin, Justin. (1999) 150 totally terrific writing prompts. NY: Scholastic Professional Books.

McLaurin, Thad H. ((1999) 730 journal prompts: grades 4-8. Greensboro, NC: The Education Center, Inc.

Senn, J.A. (1992) 325 creative prompts for personal journals. NY: Scholastic, Inc.

Picture Book Resources

Addy, Sharon Hart. (1990). Right here on this spot. NY: Houghton Mifflin.

Adler, David. (1999). The babe and i. Fairbanks, Alaska: Gulliver Books.

Auch, Mary Jane and Herm. (2002). The princess and the pizza. NY: Holiday House.

Banyai, Istvan. (1995). Zoom. NY: Viking.

Barrett, Judi. (2001). Things that are most in the world. London: Aladdin.

Blake, Robert. (2002). Togo. NY: Philomel Books.

Blume, Judy. (1974). The pain and the great one. Manchester, UK: Dell Dragonfly Books.

Bordon, Louise. (2004). The a+ custodian. London: Margaret K. McElderry.

Bruchac, Joseph. (1996). Between earth and sky: legends of native american sacred places. NY: Voyager Books.

Buzzeo, Toni. (2002). The sea chest. NY: Dial Books.

Bunting, Eve. (1999). Butterfly house. NY: Scholastic Press.

Bunting, Eve. (1999). The wall. Boston: Clarion Books.

Carlstrom, Nancy White. (1993). How does the wind walk. NY: MacMillan Publishing.

Cooney, Barbara. (1999). Basket moon. Boston: Little, Brown Publishing.

Danneberg, Julie. (2000). First day jitters. Watertown, MA: Whispering Coyote/Charlesbridge.

Dengler, Marianna. (1999). Fiddlin' sam. Flagstaff, AZ: Rising Moon Books.

Dengler, Marianna. (1996). The worry stone. Flagstaff, AZ: Rising Moon/Northland.

Dunlap, Julie. (2002). Louisa may and mr. thoreau's flute. NY: Dial Books.

Fletcher, Ralph. (2003). Hello, harvest moon. NY: MacMillan Publishing.

Flournoy, Valerie. (1985). The patchwork quilt. NY: Dial Books.

Fox, Mem. (1985). Wilfrid gordon mcdonald partridge. LaJolla, CA: Kane/Miller.

Frasier, Debra. (2000). Miss alaineus, a vocabulary disaster. NY: Harcourt.

Freeman, Don. (1975). Will's quill (or how a goose saved shakespeare. NY: Viking.

Friedman, Ina. (1984). How my parents learned to eat. NY: Houghton Mifflin.

Friedrich, Elizabeth. (1996). Leah's pony. Honesdale, PA: Boyds Mills Press.

Gibbons, Gail. (2006). Ice cream: the full scoop. NY: Holiday House.

Harshman, Marc. (1995). The storm. NY: Bobblehill Books/Dutton.

Laminack, Lester. (1998). The sunsets of miss olivia wiggins. Atlanta, GA: Peachtree.

Lang, Glenna. (2001). Looking out for sarah. Watertown, MA: Talewinds.

Lawson, Julie. (1998). Emma and the silk train. NY: Kids Can Press LTD.

Lithgow, John. (2000). The remarkable farkle mcbride. London: Simon & Schuster.

Logan, Claudia. (2002). The 5,000-year-old puzzle. NY: Melanie Kroupa Books.

McMahon, Patricia. (2005). Just add one chinese sister. Honesdale, PA: Boyds Mills Press.

Mills, Lauren. (1991). The rag coat. Boston: Little Brown.

Mendez, Phil. (1989). The black snowman. NY: Scholastic.

Mollel, Tololwa. (1999). My rows and piles of coins. Boston: Clarion Books.

Munson, Derek. (2000). Enemy pie. San Francisco: Chronicle Books LLC.

Nolan, Dennis. (1990). Dinosaur dream. London: Aladdin Paperbacks.

Older, Jules. (1997). Cow. Watertown, PA: Charlesbridge.

Older, Jules. (2004). Pig. Watertown, PA: Charlesbridge.

Park, Frances and Ginger. (2000). The royal bee. Honesdale, PA: Boyds Mills Press.

Peet, Bill. (1970). The wump world. NY: Houghton Mifflin.

Pinkney, Gloria. (1994). The sunday outing. NY: Penguin Group.

Polacco, Patricia. (2002). When lightning comes in a jar. NY: Philomel Books.

Pinkney, Andrea. (2003). Fishing day. NY: Houghton Mifflin.

Polacco, Patricia. (1996). I can hear the sun. NY: Philomel Books.

Pulver, Robin. (2003). Punctuation takes a vacation. NY: Holiday House.

Ransom, Candice. (1995). When the whippoorwill calls. NY: Tambourine Books.

Red, Yellow, Green and Blue. (2001). The official m & m's history of chocolate. Watertown, MA: Charlesbridge.

Rohmann, Eric. (1994). Time flies. NY: Crown.

Rylant, Cynthia. (1996). The old woman who named things. NY: Harcourt Brace.

Ryan, Pam Munoz. (2001). Hello ocean. Watertown, MA: Talewinds.

Schachner, Judy. (2003). Skippyjon jones. NY: Puffin Books.

Seuss, Dr. (1998). Hooray for diffendoofer day. NY: Alfred A. Knopf, Inc.

Solheim, James. (1998). It's disgusting—and we ate it. NY: Scholastic.

Spinelli, Eileen. (1993). Boy, can he dance. New Zealand: Four Winds Press.

Stanley, Diane. (1997). Rumpelstiltskin's daughter. NY: Morrow Junior Books.

Steig, William. (1990). Shrek. NY: Farrar, Straus, and Giroux.

Steig, William. (1976). The amazing bone. NY: Farrar, Straus & Giroux.

Steig, William. (1969). Sylvester and the magic pebble. London: Simon & Schuster.

Stewart, Sara. (2001). The journey. NY: Farrar, Straus, Giroux.

St. George, Judith. (2000). So you want to be president? NY: Scholastic.

Taylor, Sean. (2004). Boing! Cambridge, MA: Candlewick.

Toft, Kim. (2005). The world that we want. Watertown, MA: Charlesbridge.

Van Allsburg, Chris. (1993). The sweetest fig. NY: Houghton Mifflin.

Van Allsburg, Chris. (1991). The wretched stone. Boston: Houghton Mifflin.

Van Allsburg, Chris. (1990). Just a dream. NY: Houghton Mifflin.

Vizurraga, Susan. (1997). Our old house. NY: H. Holt Publishing.

Van Allsburg, Chris. (1986. The stranger. Boston: Houghton Mifflin.

Viortst, Judith. (1978). Alexander, who used to be rich last sunday. London: Atheneum.

Viorst, Judith. (1990). Earrings. NY: Simon and Schuster.

Weller, Frances. (1990). Riptide. South Pasadena, CA: Sandcastle Publishing & Distribution.

Weisner, David. (1992). June 29, 1999. NY: Clarion Books.

Williams, Margery. (1958). The velveteen rabbit. Manchester, UK: Dragonfly Books.

Zahares, Wade. (2001). Big bad and a little bit scary. NY: Viking.

Internet Resources

The following Internet sites were active at the time of this printing.

Alaska Department of Education, Alaska Comprehensive System of Student Assessment, 2006.
http://www.eed.state.ak.us/tls/assessment/sba

California Department of Education, Writing Prompt and Response Booklet, 2005. http://www.cde.ca.gov

Florida Department of Education. FCAT Writing Rubric. 2004.
http://apps.sdhc.k12.fl.us/sdhc2/elementary/languagearts/fcat_writerubric.htm

Georgia Department of Education, Office of Curriculum and Instruction, 2005-2006.
http://public.doe.k12.ga.us

Illinois State Board of Education, Student Assessment Framework: Writing, 2006.
http://www.isbe.net/assessment/writing.htm

Kentucky Department of Education, Sample Released Questions with Annotated Student Responses, 2004.
http://www.education.ky.gov/kde.html

Mary Jane Moffat's Journal Prompts, DeAnza College. 2006.
http://faculty.deanza.fhda.edu/jocalo/stories/storyReader$1037

Mississippi Department of Education, Mississippi Grade Level Testing Program, 2006.
http://www.mde.k12.ms.us

Nancy Polette's Children's Literature Site. 1999-2006 Picture Books. 2006
http://www.nancypolette.com/picturesbooks)Spring2006.asp

NCTE Guideline: NCTE Beliefs about the Teaching of Writing. 2004.
http://www.ncte.org/about/over/positions/category/write/118876.htm

Nevada Department of Education, Six-trait Analytical Writing Assessment Model, 2006.
http://www.doe.nv.gov/statetesting/writingassess.html#sixtrait

New York Public Library. 100 Picture Books Everyone Should Know. 2006.
http://kids.nypl.org/reading/recommended1.cfm?ListID=61

North Carolina Public Schools, North Carolina Writing Assessment, 2005.
http://www.ncpublicschools.org/docs/accountability/testing/writing

Ohio Department of Education. Testing and Assessments, 2006.
http://www.ode.state.oh.us/GD/

Oregon Department of Education, Using Sample Prompts Writing, Traits of good writing, 2006.
http://www.ode.state.or.us

Pieces of Learning, product web site www.piecesoflearning.com

State of Delaware, DSTP Sample test items—Delaware Department of Education, 2006.
http://www.doe.k12.de.us/info/sbe

State of Indiana Department of Education, Indiana Academic Standards for Language Arts, 2005.
http://www.doe.state.in.us

State of Indiana Department of Education, Teacher's Scoring Guide ISTEP+: Grades 3-6/McGraw-Hill, Monterey, CA. 2005.

State of Michigan Department of Education. Michigan Educational Assessment Program, 2006.
http://www.michigan.gov/mde

State of Utah Office of Education, Utah State office of Education: Assessment & Accountability, 2006.
http://www.usoe.k12.ut.us

Stockton-San Joaquin County Public Library. 100 Best Picture Books. 2006.
http://www.stockton.lib.ca.us/features/booklists/pictbook.html

Tennessee Department of Education, Assessment, Evaluation and Research, 2004-2005.
http://www.state.tn.us/education/assessment/tswriting

Texas Statewide Assessment. TAKS: Texas Assessment of Knowledge and Skills, 2006.
http://www.doe.state.in.us/mmp/pdf/migrant_taks.pdf

University of Waikato. 100 Essential Picture Books for Primary Schools. 2006.
http://www.waikato.ac.nz/library/resources/edu/booklst_100ess.shtml

Virginia Department of Education, Virginia Standards of Learning Assessments, 2005.
http://www.pen.k12.va.us

Washington Office of Superintendent of Public Instruction, Washington Assessment of Student Learning (WASL) in Writing, 2006.
http://www.k12.wa.us/assessment

West Virginia Department of Education, Writing Assessment Administration Manual, 2006.
http://www.wvde.state.wv.us

Your Florida Department of Education, Assessment and School Performance, 2006.
http://www.firn.edu/doe/sas